RUTH BURROWS

RUTH BURROWS

Essential Writings

Selected with an Introduction by

MICHELLE JONES

ORBIS BOOKS

Maryknoll, New York 10545

ORBIS BOOKS
Maryknoll, New York 10545

Fathers and Brothers
MARYKNOLL™

Founded in 1970, Orbis Books endeavors to publish works that enlighten the mind, nourish the spirit, and challenge the conscience. The publishing arm of the Maryknoll Fathers and Brothers, Orbis seeks to explore the global dimensions of the Christian faith and mission, to invite dialogue with diverse cultures and religious traditions, and to serve the cause of reconciliation and peace. The books published reflect the views of their authors and do not represent the official position of the Maryknoll Society. To learn more about Maryknoll and Orbis Books, please visit our website at www.maryknollsociety.org.

Library of Congress Cataloging-in-Publication Data

Names: Burrows, Ruth, author. | Jones, Michelle, 1976- editor.
Title: Ruth Burrows : essential writings / selected with an introduction by Michelle Jones.
Description: Maryknoll : Orbis Books, 2019. | Series: Modern spiritual masters series | Includes bibliographical references.
Identifiers: LCCN 2018041096 (print) | LCCN 2018055152 (ebook) | ISBN 9781608337750 (ebook) | ISBN 9781626983120 (pbk.)
Subjects: LCSH: Spirituality—Catholic Church. | Spiritual life—Catholic Church.
Classification: LCC BX2350.65 (ebook) | LCC BX2350.65 .B88 2019 (print) | DDC
248—dc23
LC record available at https://lccn.loc.gov/2018041096

Contents

Sources

AL   *Ascent to Love: The Spiritual Teaching of St. John of the Cross*. London: Darton, Longman and Todd, 1987. Denville, NJ: Dimension, 1992.

BLG   *Before the Living God*. London: Sheed and Ward, 1975. New ed., London: Continuum, 2008. Mahwah, NJ: Paulist, 2008.

EP   *Essence of Prayer*. London: Burns and Oates, 2006. Mahwah, NJ: Paulist, 2006.

GMP   *Guidelines for Mystical Prayer*. London: Sheed and Ward, 1976. Denville, NJ: Dimension, 1980. New ed., London: Continuum, 2007. Mahway, NJ: Paulist, 2017.

GW   "Prayer Is God's Work." Interview by Amy Frykholm. *The Christian Century*, April 4, 2012, 10–11.

ICE   *Interior Castle Explored: St. Teresa's Teaching on the Life of Deep Union with God*. London: Sheed and Ward, 1981. New ed., London: Continuum, 2007. Mahwah, NJ: Paulist, 2007.

IP   "Initial Prayer within the Carmelite Tradition." *Mount Carmel* 48, no. 3 (October–December 2000): 14–18.

LL   *Living Love: Meditations on the New Testament*. London: Darton, Longman and Todd, 1985. Denville, NJ: Dimension, 1985.

LM   *Living in Mystery*. London: Sheed and Ward, 1996.

LP   With Mark Allen. *Letters on Prayer: An Exchange on Prayer and Faith*. London: Sheed and Ward, 1999.

LU   *Love Unknown: Archbishop of Canterbury's Lent Book 2012*. London: Continuum, 2011.

LY   "Lose Yourself: Getting Past 'Me' to 'Thee.'" *America*, December 23, 2013, 19–20.

MS   "Manuscript." Quidenham. Unpublished manuscript. (Document comprised of the passages omitted from the published version of *Before the Living God*).

OF   *Our Father: Meditations on the Lord's Prayer*. London: Darton, Longman and Todd, 1986. Denville, NJ: Dimension, 1986.

OnF   "On Formation." Quidenham. Unpublished article.

QUD   *Quis Ut Deus? Who Is as God? Meditations on the Kenosis of the Son of God*. Quidenham, 2013. Unpublished manuscript.

SH   "Smile Though Your Heart Is Aching." *The Tablet*, April 19, 2014, 10–11.

TBJ   *To Believe in Jesus*. London: Sheed and Ward, 1978. New ed., London: Continuum, 2010. Mahwah, NJ: Paulist, 2010.

TH   *Through Him, with Him, in Him: Meditations on the Liturgical Seasons*. London: Sheed and Ward, 1987. Denville, NJ: Dimension, 1987.

Acknowledgments

My loving thanks to Sr. Rachel and all the Sisters of the Quidenham Carmelite Community, along with Sr. Wendy Beckett, for their prayerful support and for providing me with a spiritual home. I am also very grateful to Fr. Stephen Sundborg, SJ, for so generously sharing his extensive research with me. Finally, I thank my dear friend Fr. Charles Waddell for being a wise and patient sounding board as I prepared this work.

Grateful acknowledgment is made to the following publishers for permission to reprint previously published material:

To Paulist Press (Mahwah, NJ) for selections from *To Believe in Jesus* © 2010; *Essence of Prayer* © 2006; *Interior Castle Explored* © 2007; *Before the Living God* © 2008; and *Guidelines for Mystical Prayer* © 2017. This limited edition licensed by special permission of Paulist Press, Inc. www.paulistpress.com.

To Bloomsbury Publishing (London) for selections from *Through Him, With Him, In Him: Meditations on the Liturgical Seasons* © 1997; *Living in Mystery* © 1996; *Letters on Prayer: An Exchange on Prayer and Faith* © 1999; *Love Unknown* © 2011; and for distribution in the Commonwealth, *To Believe in Jesus* © 2010; *Essence of Prayer* © 2006; *Before the Living God* © 2008; *Guidelines for Mystical Prayer* © 2007; *Interior Castle Explored* © 2007.

To Darton, Longman, & Todd (London) for selections from *Living Love: Meditations on the New Testament* © 1985; *Our Father: Meditations on the Lord's Prayer* © 1986; *Ascent to Love: The Spiritual Teachings of St. John of the Cross* © 1987.

To the Sisters of Jesus of Nazareth, Zimbabwe, for selections from the unpublished manuscript, *Quis Ut Deus*.

To *Mount Carmel* for selections from Ruth Burrows, "Initial Prayer in the Carmelite Tradition," *Mount Carmel* 48, no. 3 (Oct-Dec 2000), 14-18.

To America Media for Ruth Burrows, "Lose Yourself: Getting Past 'Me' to 'Thee,'" *America*, December 23, 2013, 19-20.

To *Christian Century* for "Prayer is God's Work: Interview with Ruth Burrows" by Amy Frykholm, copyright © 2012 by *The Christian Century*, April 4, 2012.

To *The Tablet* for Ruth Burrows, "Smile though your heart is aching," *The Tablet* (The International Catholic News Weekly), April 19, 2014, 10-11. http://www.thetablet.co.uk

To Sister M. Caritas Müller, OP, for permission to reprint "The Merciful Trinity."

Introduction:
To Know the Gift of God

In an unpublished section of her autobiography, *Before the Living God*, Ruth Burrows writes, "If one measures experience merely by such things as the number of countries one has visited, jobs one has held down and so on, then my experience is nil. But if it is measured by penetration into life, into human nature, then mine is great." A brief survey of her long life reveals that it is indeed unusually circumscribed in its outward scope.

Rachel Gregory—"Ruth Burrows" is her pen name—was born in Sheffield, England, on August 18, 1923. She was the third of seven children of Edmund and Elsie Gregory. The eldest child and "flower of the flock" (*BLG*, 13), Margaret, died in childhood. Family life was shaped by the beliefs and practices of the Catholic faith, and Rachel and her siblings attended Catholic primary and secondary schools.

Soon after her eighteenth birthday, in the September of 1941, Rachel left the home in which she had grown up and traveled by bus to a Carmelite monastery in Mansfield. She had turned down an offer of a place at Oxford in order to become a nun. Rachel's account of her departure from home is poignant in its ordinariness and humanity.

> After lunch Mother said gently: "I should get off now dear, there is no point in hanging about." I knew the heroism behind this sentence. She was trying to save me pain. . . . She kissed me in a matter-of-fact way as if I were going to school. I looked around for Daddy but he was not there. Thinking he would be tinkering with the

1

car, I went down the little path. I heard a broken cry and turning round saw him in the doorway with his arms wide open the tears streaming down his cheeks. I ran back and flung myself into his arms. He clutched me to himself in a wild, passionate hug, kissing me over and over. Mother intervened in her gentle way and released me from his grip. And so I left home in a sort of trance. (*BLG*, 40)

Sister Rachel has lived as an enclosed Carmelite nun to this day. In 1948, the Mansfield community relocated to the rural location of Ashbourne, and twelve years later it moved again to amalgamate with the Carmelite community at Quidenham in Norfolk; in time, a third Carmelite community was incorporated into this amalgam. Rachel has served her community over many decades as prioress and as novice mistress. As prioress, she played a pivotal and ground-breaking role in reforming the Quidenham Carmel in response to the directives of the Second Vatican Council. Indeed, it has been said that Rachel "has done more than any other one person for the Teresian nuns in England during the post-Vatican II period."[1] Rachel is known beyond the Carmelite world through her writings. Her first book, *Before the Living God*, was published in 1975. Since then, she has written twelve other books and many articles on the Christian life in general and the Carmelite spiritual tradition in particular. We will return to Rachel's influential leadership and her writings shortly.

From within her circumscribed and intensely focused existence, Rachel has plumbed the depths of the significance of life. In the words of former Archbishop of Canterbury Rowan Williams, "It is a history that has the effect of providing a definition of faith itself in terms of radical conversion to the perspective

---

1. Elizabeth Ruth Obbard, review of *Carmel: Interpreting a Great Tradition*, by Ruth Burrows, *Bulletin, Our Lady of the Assumption: British Province of Carmelites* 31, no. 8 (Winter 2001): 11.

of the indwelling Christ" (Introduction, *BLG*, ix). The hermit and art critic Sister Wendy Beckett elaborates, "There are very few writers who understand the Mystery of God and the absoluteness with which Jesus has shared with us all he is. Julian of Norwich understands . . . and so does St. Teresa of Avila and St. Thérèse of Lisieux. To these names we can add another, Ruth Burrows" (Foreword, *LM*, vii).

This "penetration into life" has emerged from Rachel's steadfast refusal to evade her painful inner reality. As we shall see in the passages ahead, since childhood, Rachel has known a singularly raw exposure to the dependency and vulnerability at the root of human existence. She opens *Before the Living God* by revealing, "I was born into this world with a tortured sensitivity" (*BLG*, 5). Developing this image elsewhere, she describes herself as having been "born with her eyes open," able to see "behind life's façade to its ugliness and grief" (*GMP*, 109).

Rachel's birth was, indeed, traumatic. She wonders if she may even remember it. "My dreams as a child were terrifying," she recounts. "The prevailing one was of hurtling, sliding down a green, slimy, dark abyss. Was this a memory of birth itself?" Certainly, Rachel does know, "my birth was difficult and [my mother] was ill. I was put aside and, to use her own word, 'neglected,' while attention was given to her" (*BLG*, 6). This inadvertent neglect continued into Rachel's infancy. Looking back, she ponders,

> My position in the family was unfavorable for an over-sensitive child. Little more than twelve months divided us children from one another. When I came on the scene my mother already had her hands full. I was just twelve months old when James was born. The stage of intense cuddling was over for me then. I suspect that I needed more than my ordinary share and possibly received less than the others. (*BLG*, 6)

Living with such extreme sensitivity to life's fragility has meant that Rachel has suffered from profound and relentless anxiety. As a child, this blight took such shapes as terror of being mauled by lions and tigers, or of being kidnapped, or of bridges and staircases collapsing. In her adolescence, the intense anxiety was expressed as depression, moodiness, fits of rage, and self-loathing. In time, she attempted to minimize the distress her moods inflicted on her family, all the while sadly aware that "no one in my really loving home grasped the inner loneliness of the difficult child that was me" (*BLG*, 26).

The images of God with which Rachel was presented during her early years made no impression on her. Certainly, they were powerless to assuage her terrifying vulnerability to life's fragility. Reflecting on her youth she writes, "Often I have complained in my heart that God seemed absent from my life. It seemed to me that I had to live life all alone, eating it in its raw bitterness. He was not there to give me understanding and comfort. Even now I can sympathize with myself over this" (*BLG*, 31). The spiritual awakening that occurred on a school retreat during her seventeenth year, which contained her call to Carmel, imprinted her depths indelibly with the realization that God existed and that it was possible to be intimate with God. However, God remained "totally remote" from her (*BLG*, 36); "prayer as always was utterly blank" (*BLG*, 54).

Rachel's existential anxiety and black depression accompanied her across the threshold of Carmel and only tightened their grip as the years unfolded. For many years she continued to be bereft of any human or divine consolation. The situation into which Rachel entered was bleakly austere in its physical hardships and penitential traditions, and dysfunctional in its leadership, approach to religious formation, and community life. She was unable to escape the effect of her conversion experience, yet she paradoxically had to bear the unremitting sense of God's absence. Rachel yearned for "inside" prayer, for union with the living God, yet the spiritual practices she was taught seemed to keep God "outside" of her deepest self. "There was not the slightest gleam, not the slightest thought that made any impression on me or feeling that touched me" (*BLG*, 51).

Rachel experienced herself to be a living contradiction and a failure. She was at once irresistibly drawn to and repulsed by life in Carmel. "Hating the life which was [God's] choice" felt like sin (*BLG*, 55), and this feeling was only compounded by her frequent failures to meet the demands of charity presented by daily monastic life, not to mention the total nothingness of her experience in prayer. "It is easy to vaunt one's 'poverty,' 'wretchedness,' and so forth," Rachel relates, "but truly, I cannot convey how unremitting and painful was the awareness of my sinfulness and spiritual helplessness. On the level of normal perception, I was a complete failure. It would have been impossible to communicate the reality of it to another, even had I dared to do so!" (*LU*, 6).

Rachel's fathomless existential vulnerability, which left her "shrieking with loneliness and pain" (*BLG*, 109) and feeling powerless to face life, is the ground from which her universal insights, her penetration into life, emerged. She gradually discovered that despite all indications to the contrary at the surface level, this raw nothingness is the very place where Jesus dwelt and uttered his self-emptying "Yes" to the Father's outpoured love. While conventional wisdom would tell her somehow to get a grip, the secret was rather to abide empty-handed in Jesus, in him surrendering her poverty to God in trust.

We will see the emergence of this discovery in Chapter 1. It was largely facilitated by Rachel's persistent meditation on the New Testament; this had been a habit, she tells us, "almost from the beginning of my serious discipleship" (*LU*, 7). Radically identifying with every needy person Jesus encountered, she began to see her neediness as the means through which Jesus would be the way, the truth, and the life in her. She did not have to take herself to God, but rather Jesus would continue the incarnation through her as she entrusted to him her fragile humanity. Rachel also found theological texts that reinforced this fundamental biblical insight. She read that in assuming our human condition, Jesus descended into the depths of our frightening contingency and alienation from God and that the crucified and risen Jesus, knowing no limits, is now able truly to "inhabit" our inner reality. The writings of St. Thérèse of Lisieux, with her confident insistence that we must "love to feel nothing" and "love our littleness" because this disposes us to the descending love of God,[2] also nurtured Rachel's growth in understanding.

In time, Rachel discerned that the mystical teachings of the Carmelite "giants"—St. Teresa of Avila and St. John of the Cross—were essentially the same as the Gospel pattern imprinted on her poor, barren life. Earlier in her religious life, Rachel felt estranged from these towering mystical figures, convinced that their lofty lives and writings were utterly removed from her inner world of fragility and failure. Additionally, for many years, discourse on mysticism in general repelled her: "I couldn't bear the word and eschewed discussion of it. But that was precisely because it seemed to me to be unrelated to Jesus, to be seen as something cultivated, a fascinating possibility, something that gave promise of a wonderful experience" (GMP, 2).

But Rachel questioned, "Why should Teresa be a seraph when Jesus was not?" (ICE, 3). In other words, she reasoned that there could not be any other measure of the spiritual life than the Gospel. If Teresa, John, or anyone else is to be lauded as a mystic, it can only mean that "Jesus [is] living in [them], self drained away" (GMP, 3). And such self-emptying is not seraphic, but rather brings one face to face with the vulnerability and dependency of the human condition. Thus, Rachel can ruminate, "It is born in on me more as the years go by, how profound is this theme of human helplessness and our loving acceptance of it. It is truly mystical" (TBJ, 41–42).

As for the seraphic, the exalted experiences traditionally associated with mysticism, with the heights of the spiritual life, Rachel came to perceive that they must be viewed through the lens of modern psychological insights. What former eras saw as indubitable signs of the divine presence and favor, we must now

---

2. Letter from Thérèse to Sister Marie of the Sacred Heart, September 17, 1896, in St. Thérèse of Lisieux, *General Correspondence*, vol. 2: 1890–1897, trans. John Clarke (Washington, DC: ICS Publications, 1988), 999.

have the courage and clarity to see as phenomena "rising out of the psyche under certain stimuli" (*GMP*, 50). They may be echoes of the touch of God but, as a contemporary appreciation of the realm of the psyche clarifies, they "could just as easily come from other sources" (*TBJ*, 28).

As she entered mid-life Rachel began to recognize that others might benefit from her sharing the lights arising from her ever-dark lived experience. She was encouraged in this realization by Sister Wendy Beckett, who in 1971 moved to Quidenham to live as a hermit within the grounds of the Carmelite monastery; Wendy soon became the friend and spiritual confidant for which Rachel had long yearned. Rachel came to accept that her acute sensitivity to life's dreadful precariousness had led her to an absolute expression of the trust we all must have before the living God. Jesus proclaims, "No one comes to the Father except through me" (John 14:6), and Rachel's unmitigated desolation left her with no alternative but to be taken to God in Jesus. She indicates the revelatory character of her surrendered fragility in an analogy:

> It is easier for some natures to trust God than for others. They have a basic security and, in spite of difficulties, life is experienced as good. But for others of a less robust and solid structure it is much more difficult. If a pewter mug and an egg shell china cup were conscious, their experiences would be very different. The latter would live with a sense of peril. So the fragile nature has no natural foundation for trust and when it truly trusts in God its trust is pure. The more solid nature cannot know how authentic is its trust in God until its inner security is taken away and it is reduced to a similar state of deprivation and fragility. (*LM*, 101)

Indeed, by this stage of her life, Rachel's reforming leadership of the Quidenham community had made her well-established in exercising influence. She had always known a "powerful, creative nature" alongside her "shrinking sensibility" (*BLG*, 19). In

her last year of school, Rachel was chosen as the head girl, and
the principal of the time would later relate that she had never
seen a girl have such a transformative impact on her peers. "I
have some very happy memories of that last year at school,"
Rachel reflects. "Beautiful human fellowship, union of heart and
mind, real love and a flowering of virtues such as truth, honor,
kindness, respect for one another, appreciation and gratitude. I
saw characters expand. In all truth I have to say that I was aware
of the role I had played in this" (*BLG*, 38). It was not long after
entering Carmel that she perceived she "had a natural ascendancy" among the sisters (*BLG*, 45). And when, at a relatively
young age, she was appointed novice mistress, and soon after
prioress, she admitted to desiring and feeling well suited to the
positions, even though the prevailing mentality was that "such
a one was the last person to be governing others" (*BLG*, 103).

As I indicated earlier, through her leadership Rachel imple-
mented the reforming spirit of the Second Vatican Council.
More fundamentally, she set about correcting the dysfunction
she had hitherto experienced in Carmel:

> The first thing I wanted to do was to make the sisters
> happy. I wanted to create such an atmosphere of mutual
> trust between the prioress and the sisters and among the
> sisters themselves—I saw how much the latter depended
> on the former—that each one would have the uncon-
> scious security of being valued, trusted and loved. . . .
> Only in an atmosphere of acceptance can a person
> reveal herself as she is, and thus grow in understanding
> of herself and be open to development (*BLG*, 103–4).

As expressed in her unpublished article "On Formation," in
renewing the community's approach to formation, Rachel recognized that "each person is different and each must be guided
differently" (*OnF*, 1). Moreover, formation should promote
full human flourishing. "Mary Jones remains Mary Jones, she
doesn't doff Mary Jones and put on the persona of a 'postulant.'
I want her to 'feel' herself as Mary Jones living in a convent. It

is Mary Jones who is to be transformed into Christ. Mary Jones must become more and more Mary Jones as she submits to the way of life she undertakes" (*OnF*, 1). To this end, Rachel has encouraged innovations such as the fostering of personal gifts and a wide range of reading, reasoning that "anything which develops us as persons opens us to God" (*OnF*, 5). Such developments in the enclosed Carmelite life, along with Rachel's leadership in the reformation of other "archaic and ridiculous" aspects of her community's way of life (*BLG*, 106–7) have not been without criticism from the wider Carmelite family.

Everything Rachel has conveyed to others through her writings over the past five decades flows from her lived experience, and carries the radiance and authority of this experience. A comment Rachel made to the Jesuit priest Stephen Sundborg, who, through his doctoral thesis, was the first person to write about Rachel in a systematic way, points to the continuity between her life and writings. "What my books are saying is pure Jesus—nothing else, but a Jesus poor, threadbare, a Jesus who is nothing but himself and wants to be accepted thus. And this Jesus can unite himself to us only if we consent to become like him—without beauty, glory, grandeur."[3] While made in 1979, this declaration is applicable to Rachel's writings to date.

Rachel adopted the pen-name of "Ruth Burrows" for *Before the Living God* and also altered dates and events within her life story. She also mixed up names and personalities in order to protect the privacy of the people she mentions. These veils of obscurity freed Rachel to write with exceptional frankness, surprising—even jolting—many with revelations not expected from an enclosed nun. After publishing her autobiography, Rachel wrote *Guidelines for Mystical Prayer*. This book is more directly autobiographical than it appears. She claims that it emerged from her discussions with two nuns, "Petra" and "Claire"; the book recounts much of their own personal spiritual journeys, especially their contrasting ways of experiencing transforming

---

3. Rachel Gregory, letter to Stephen Sundborg, July 18, 1979.

union, the culmination of the spiritual journey. However, "Petra" is, in fact, Rachel herself. People had begun to discover that she was "Ruth Burrows," so Rachel used another form of obscurity in order to be transparent about her life.

Other works may appear to be purely objective, such as her presentations of the spiritual teachings of Teresa of Avila (*Interior Castle Explored*) or John of the Cross (*Ascent to Love*), or her more scripturally grounded works *To Believe in Jesus* and *Love Unknown*. Yet all is filtered through the lens of her fundamental experience of being taken into Jesus as he expresses his "Yes" to the Father's outpoured love in and through her frail humanity.

Rachel offers something of a mission statement when she writes, "There is a ruling insight that covers and controls my life and all that I would or could communicate to others. It runs through everything I have written: God offers himself in total love to each one of us. Our part is to open our hearts to receive the gift" (*LU*, 38). This statement contains the main themes of Rachel's writings. It also provides the structure for this anthology, as we will soon see. Given that Rachel's works echo her life, to discuss the themes within these works is to distill the wisdom we have seen embodied by her lived experience.

There are five interrelated themes for us to consider. First, the Christian life is about the transformation of the ego into the very life of Jesus. Rachel emphasizes throughout that we receive God's outpoured love only in Jesus, "who is close to the Father's heart, who has made him known" (John 1:18). So our hearts are to be taken into Jesus's heart where we encounter complete receptivity to God's total self-gift.

The second theme is that this transformation from egocentricity into the self-emptying life of Jesus is precisely what is meant by the mystical life. "The heart of mysticism is Jesus" (*GMP*, 4). Rachel asserts that mysticism can have nothing intrinsic to do with what is felt at the surface level of our lives. To live the mystical life is to participate in the communion of love between the Father and the Son, and this divine exchange cannot be grasped by our created faculties.

Third, the transformation of our innate self-centeredness into Jesus's receptivity to God's love encompasses every aspect of our lives. Prayer and life are continuousness, or, to use Rachel's words, "Prayer is not just one function in life, not even the most important, it is life itself. We are only truly living, truly and fully human when our whole life is prayer" (*TBJ*, 78). Prayer is God's total giving of himself in love and our response to that self-gift. We incarnate Jesus's assent to love both in our everyday turning from selfishness in our interactions with others, and in our attempts to remain in empty-handed openness to God during those times specifically set aside for "prayer."

The fourth theme is that our being taken into Jesus's life of love is a collaboration between human effort and God's grace; "perfect transformation into Jesus does not take place all at once" (*TBJ*, 31). While the uprooting of our egocentricity and the consequent blossoming in us of the life of Jesus is ultimately a divine work, the work of mystical grace, we must do what we can to pull the heads off the weeds of our self-preoccupation. In this regard, Rachel counsels daily recourse to the Gospels in order to deepen our intimacy with Jesus and to increase our desire to live in union with him. She also counsels a commitment to simple ascetical practices woven into the texture of everyday life aimed at toppling the reign of the ego.

Finally, Rachel emphasizes that we cultivate openness to God's gift of love through faith, or trust; as her friend and sister in Carmel Elizabeth Ruth Obbard neatly puts it, "Faith is worked out in daily life by a growing trust in God" (Introduction, *The Watchful Heart*, xii). Growing in trust in God necessitates growing in distrust of ourselves. So transformation into Jesus's perfect openness to the Father means progressively dropping the barricades of our own attempts at self-perfection and standing in our naked neediness before the outpoured love of God.

These themes are interwoven throughout the passages in this collection. As I mentioned, I have structured the anthology around Rachel's "mission statement." The first chapter takes us

through Rachel's discovery in her own life of the gift of God—
the total outpouring of love encountered in and through Jesus.
In the second chapter we look squarely at Rachel's understanding of God as love, longing to give himself completely to each
one of us. The counterpart of this divine self-gift is the focus of
the third chapter, where we explore Rachel's insight that to be
human is to be created to receive God's love. We learn here that
we receive God's love in Jesus and that our journey into Jesus is
a three-stage process.

Chapter 4 addresses the first stage, which is about our initial openness to living with the life of Jesus. The emphasis is
on preparing to be immersed directly into Jesus's surrender to
God's gift of love through doing what we can to dislodge the
tyranny of the ego. This preparation becomes participation in
Chapter 5, where we contemplate Rachel's thought on receiving
the gift of God's love directly into our inmost self through union
with Jesus. With the final chapter we arrive at the third and final
stage—complete transformation into Jesus. Here Rachel sets
before us life at once completely dispossessed of selfishness and
completely possessed by God's love.

In addition to Rachel's published works, I have drawn on two
unpublished sources for this collection. The first is a document
containing passages that were omitted from the published version of Rachel's autobiography; the original version of *Before
the Living God* had to be shortened due to financial constraints.
The passages I have selected reveal important developments in
Rachel's self-understanding. The second unpublished source is a
booklet entitled *Quis Ut Deus? Who Is as God? Meditations on
the Kenosis of the Son of God*. Rachel composed this series of
short reflections in 2013 for the Sisters of Jesus of Nazareth, a
religious community in Zimbabwe.

Each excerpt in the anthology inevitably takes us into the
thought-world of its source. Thus, in the passages chosen from
Rachel's writings on Teresa of Avila and John of the Cross, we
will encounter imagery such as, respectively, the Interior Castle
and the Dark Night of the Soul. However, rather than requiring

of us specialist knowledge of these authors, Rachel manages to demystify their spiritual teachings as she uses their particular terminologies to express the insights she has gained from her lived experience. In the passages from *Guidelines for Mystical Prayer*, we sometimes encounter the imagery of islands, which Rachel uses in that book. She depicts the three stages of the spiritual life as three distinct islands, with a bridge spanning the sea between the first and second islands.

Rachel's writings also inevitably reflect her own historical context. Accordingly, we will find that she often uses noninclusive gender language in her earlier works. As cultural sensitivity to this important issue has increased in recent decades, so has Rachel's; the language in her later works is generally more gender conscious.

The various passages in the pages ahead are rather like pieces of a mosaic. While they carry unique value in themselves, their complete meaning is found when they are contemplated as part of the "bigger picture." For Rachel, the whole picture can only mean Jesus, the one in whom we encounter and receive God's total self-gift.

This metaphor can be stretched a little further. The Jesus emerging from this collection is the Jesus Rachel has found upholding the brokenness of her life. As she writes in the introduction to *Before the Living God*, "Already, it seems to me, I have grasped the mystery of my life. One long searching look into my past and I see, there in its depths, the face of Christ gazing back at me" (*BLG*, 1). We can have great confidence that the Jesus we will meet through these excerpts is similarly present within us, inviting us through our messy fragility into the eternal communion of love.

1

A Personal Discovery of the Gift of God

*There is a ruling insight that covers and controls my life
and all that I would or could communicate to others. It
runs through everything I have written: God offers himself in total love to each one of us. Our part is to open
our hearts to receive the gift.* —LU, 38

*What Rachel writes flows from what she has lived. The pas-
sages in this chapter take us into the heart of Rachel's inner life
and trace the discoveries she has made there. Rachel relates the
absoluteness of her fragility and the intensity of the pain she
has known with rare and unexpected candor. So vivid and evoc-
ative is her account that the vulnerability of life, from which
we normally try to anesthetize ourselves, stands unveiled. Those
who suffer anxiety and depression may experience a particular
resonance with Rachel's story. Indeed, Rachel tells us that as she
traversed the path of life, "I began to see that I was but one of
many who suffered from depression, the inability to face life,
fear, the sense of God's absence" (BLG, 96).*

*Rachel's life and writings give us immense hope because she
has found veins of eternal life in the dark, yearning caverns
within her. In lifelong faithfulness to the grace she received as a
teenager at the moment of her conversion, and without any support from her emotions, Rachel has never ceased to turn within*

to the hidden God who drew her to himself. She has mined and clings to the truth that through the Incarnation, Jesus entered into the full extent of humanity's frightening poverty and dependency. Trusting in the Father, he descended into the depths, even unto death, and he has emerged, breathing words of assurance and peace. So, in faith, Rachel realizes that wherever she looks within the bleakness of her inner landscape, she finds Jesus, sharing her desolation. And her emptiness is pure capacity for the inundation of God's life and love if, in Jesus, she surrenders it to him in trust.

The words with which Rachel ends her autobiography launch us well into this chapter:

> My poor, drab, little life! And yet I see it suffused with the radiance of God. Mine is but the common experience, but the common experience understood. If others should read this account of my life. . . . I hope they will find encouragement and, recognizing the marvelous works of God in their own life, cry out from their hearts with me:
>
> "My God, I thank you for the glory of my life" (BLG, 118).

A TORTURED SENSITIVITY

In these passages, Rachel reveals to us her singularly stark exposure to the insecurity and anxiety of human existence and the fundamental chasm between humanity and God.

I was born into this world with a tortured sensitivity. For long I have puzzled over the causes of my psychological anguish. I think the explanation in great part lies in heredity, possibly aggravated by circumstances. I will try to clarify this.

I must speak of my dear parents. It would be impossible to express how deeply I loved them, with a love which refused to take notice of faults or flaws even though I knew they were there. To me they were "Mother" and "Daddy" and those words were weighted with indefinable emotions of trust, love, sureness of keeping. Not until I was an adult could I bear to look on them objectively and estimate them as human persons. This is my story, not theirs, so I will say no more than is relevant.

My mother recognized the tortured side of me but was completely incapable of entering into it, as no doubt she was incapable of understanding it in my father. There was nothing hard about my mother. She was an ocean of tenderness. I am sure she suffered numbly and dumbly before the suffering which was such a mystery to her. I think one of the reasons why she "hit out" at times was just her own pain at seeing herself helpless to help. As for my dear father, I am sure he did not understand himself and had not come to terms with himself. A man of his generation and class had neither time nor opportunity for being sensitive and still less for the luxury of self-analysis. I am sure he was a painful mystery to himself. To all appearances he was a strong man, very much head of the family. As a child I felt utterly safe when Daddy was around and terrified when he was out of the house. In my early childhood he was the embodiment of safety. The rude awakening did not come until the outbreak of war when I realized that he was, now, powerless to protect us. Yet underneath this exterior was a quivering sensitivity like my own, probably all the more painful in that it was concealed from him and its manifestations must have been inexplicable and humiliating. It is a pain to me now that I did not understand him better. I was the one who could have helped him. As it was, much as I loved him, I had no real intimacy with him.

I, third child of a family of eight, seemed to unite in myself the two sharply differing temperaments of my parents. I suspect that each faced in me the mystery of the other which left each suffering. As I have said, I am sure my mother could not comprehend the manifestations of my father's sensitivity. Not comprehending them she would misinterpret them. On his side my father would shrink from showing her his hidden fears even if he were aware of them. They loved one another deeply, of that I have no doubt, and time was to reveal it unambiguously, but inevitably there

were tensions, tensions which reached a climax when I was six-
teen. This state of tension aggravated my inborn fears.

Also, my position in the family was unfavorable for an over-
sensitive child. Little more than twelve months divided us children from one another. When I came on the scene my mother
already had her hands full. I was just twelve months old when
James was born. The stage of intense cuddling was over for
me then. I suspect that I needed more than my ordinary share
and possibly received less than the others. Was it that I seemed
reserved and independent? I can remember looking on, not with
jealousy—(I cannot remember feeling jealous of any member
of my family. I think the deep tenderness which bound me in
the flesh to my brothers and sisters ruled out the possibility of
jealousy. They were part of me)—but with longing. I longed to
be cuddled and hugged. Looking back on my childhood I must
single out fear as the preponderating emotion as far as I can
recall. My dreams as a child were terrifying. The prevailing one
was of hurtling, sliding down a green, slimy, dark abyss. Was
this a memory of birth itself? My mother told me that my birth
was difficult and that she was ill. I was put aside and, to use her
own word, "neglected," while attention was given to her. There
is something awe inspiring in recalling the moment of one's
birth. Human birth! I wish I could speak adequately of this deep
mystery. I can do nothing but recall the unutterable wonder that
God too had a human birth: he came into the world as we come
into it; he came to drink with us the bitter cup of humanness.
He drank it to the dregs and thereby transformed its bitterness.
Bitter it is still and yet sweet, for his lips meet ours over the brim.

For me there were bogeys hidden in every dark corner, in
everything untested and untried. I would scream and kick with
terror when, quite unwittingly, those in charge of me introduced
me to some new experience. I was a lively child, bright and gay.
Suddenly, inexplicably, in the midst of gaiety, I would dissolve
into a flood of tears. Mine were not quiet, unobtrusive ones. On
the contrary, they were vociferous and accompanied by fight-
ing, spitting, scratching. Looking back I would say that almost

always my tantrums were nothing but fear and wounded sensitivity. Someone unthinkingly trod on my toes; a sense of menace, perhaps due to a passing cloud or a darkening atmosphere,
would suddenly descend on me. In my defenselessness I reacted
with violent storms.   —*BLG*, 5–7

I had sent a snapshot of myself as a child of seven or eight to
Elsa, my friend and counsellor. Elsa responded: This is a child
made for tears, a child naked to reality, suffering, bewildered,
quivering, a pathetic smile to propitiate the mystery round her.
A small, closed world of fear and pain.   —*LM*, 11

I was seven years old when I made my first confession and first
communion. They made little or no impression on me. . . . Others have told me that God was very real to them in their childhood. I cannot say the same. I knew my catechism and shone
at answering all questions on confession, the Mass and Holy
Communion, but so far as I know it was not in my heart. Here
already is that dryness which has been my lot all my life.
                                                       —*BLG*, 10

Helena's death left me scarred. Later someone was to suggest
that I had never forgiven God for taking her. Forgiveness implies
a sense of personal relationship and, with God, I was conscious
of none. He was too much God for that. What is more, I never
heard from either of my parents anything to suggest that God
had wronged us, not the least complaint or note of rebellion,
only words indicating unquestioning acceptance of his will.
They turned to him for comfort and it was obvious that they
found it. I think my attitude was more like this: "Nothing is
safe anymore. Anything terrible can happen, it has happened
once and can happen again and there is no one can stop it. God
won't stop it." The menace had taken form and substance and I
connected this with God. He had not intervened to save Helena
though we had prayed to him. Indeed, it was he who had taken
her from us, everyone said so. He was a terrible God. Engraven

on my flesh was the feeling of God as the one who deprived, who was jealous of our human loves. Let me love anyone and God was sure to remove my loved one. This wound was only later healed by a friend God gave me, a friend who loved me with a deep love and in whom I have found joy. The trouble was on an emotional level and God came to me on the emotional level through friendship.   —*BLG*, 17

[T]he sheer fragility of my being. Here was existential fear, the fear of existence itself. Here was threatened, meaningless existence. Later on I was to read something of Kierkegaard and others and recognize my own state in theirs. Fr. Bernard was to exclaim: "How well you write. Far better than the existentialists themselves!" All through the years that followed, though I sought help, hoped for help in this or that, in this person or that, deep in my heart I knew there was no remedy. My suffering lay at the very roots of existence which no mortal hand could reach. And God was utterly absent.   —*BLG*, 110

GOD TURNED ME

This section begins with Rachel's descriptions of her conversion experience and her early days as a Carmelite nun. We see that after being definitively oriented to God as a teenager, Rachel has never ceased to turn within to him, despite knowing no relief from the darkness of her inner life.

Like every Catholic girl of my generation, educated at a convent school, I was aware that there was such a thing as "religious vocation" and that this was, in theory at any rate, highly esteemed. This aspect was the only one that caused the slightest flutter of my heart but it was certainly not appealing enough to turn my thoughts in the direction of a convent. Resolutely I looked toward marriage.

It was a custom in the school for the girls to make a few days retreat annually. It was to take place in the half-term holiday of Whitsun. I was furious, partly because it was taking a slice out of our coveted holiday at home but chiefly because I felt it as an imposition. The nuns had no right to force their piety on us. I resented what seemed to me an invasion of my personal privacy. They had the right to teach us in all manner of ways, but our spiritual life was no affair of theirs, I argued. However, I was too concerned for my good standing in the school and in the opinion of the nuns to stay away. Inwardly smoldering I went. Deliberately I set myself to be a nuisance. I refused to keep silent and chattered to anyone who was willing to chatter. Some of the girls were taking the retreat seriously and our chatter harassed them. I heard not a word of what the preacher said. To this day I cannot remember a single word. Quite suddenly, in the middle of the second day, I was seized with a sense of fear such as I had never known before. It was related directly to God and to him alone. "What did he think? What was I doing? Wasn't this 'resisting grace,' and how serious that was." I went home in the evening still in the grip of this profound emotion, gulped down my tea (there was rhubarb pie and custard which I loved), remarked casually to Mother that I was going off to confession and off I went.

Hitherto I had avoided going to the Canon for confession. He annoyed me with his fussy piety, but now I deliberately went to him. What instinct lay behind this? Was it that, for once, my confession was to be in deadly earnest and that I laid aside all merely personal whims and went to the most experienced priest of the three serving the parish? Something like that, I think. I told him in a very straightforward way what I had done. He asked me why I had behaved so and I replied that I was mad with the nuns. I felt they had no right to be making us pious. He asked was I sure that was the only reason; was I perhaps afraid that God was asking something of me and I didn't want to listen. I assured him quite definitely that it was simply because I was mad with the nuns. I knew what the Canon was hinting at.

I came out of the confessional with a sense of relief and peace. The priest had urged me to spend the next few days well and I was determined to do so. I thought over what he had said. Yes,

I knew quite well what he was getting at, hinting that perhaps I had a vocation. I realized that, in fact, I was afraid of being "good." That is, if once I decided to be "good" anything might happen, there would be no knowing where it would end. This was the moment for the grace which changed my life. At the deepest level of my self I *saw* that God existed. He filled life. He offered intimacy to man. It was possible for us to be intimate with God! Bewildering realization. That being so life could have no other meaning. I must give myself up to seeking this intimacy with God. The self-evident way was to be a nun, a nun in the most absolute way possible, an enclosed, contemplative nun. These successive thoughts were almost instantaneous. All happened in a moment but my mind was made up in the sort of way that it would have been impossible to unmake. My world was completely changed.

So powerful was this grace—it was not experienced in an overwhelming way, rather it was veiled in obscurity and also by a web of natural movements—that it changed me in an instant and radically. It was a real "conversion." I was turned right round. I use the passive tense deliberately. It was not I who turned. God turned me. My orientation was henceforth different, it was to him, and so fundamental, radical was this orientation that I think it would have been impossible for me to reverse it or withdraw from the powerful current which now had me in its grip. What others have to come to through steady application and labor, had been done for me in a moment. A work of detachment had been wrought for me. This was a "short-cut" such as St. Teresa [of Avila] speaks of; a mystical grace which of its very nature is efficacious. There has been no other such in my life. From then on I had to submit to the toilsome, slow climb of the ordinary way. This grace was but a beginning. It set me on the mountain, at its base, but so firmly, so surely that it has been, as I say, impossible to withdraw. It would have been necessary to unmake my fabric, so to speak, for that to happen.

But from then on and apart from that, my path lay in darkness, deep darkness; and I had to struggle bitterly for the practice of

virtue. Nothing of that was made easy. Yet I think I can say truly that, thanks to this initial grace, not for one hour have I given up the climb. I have known utter dejection and near-despair. I have known intolerable bitterness and yet never have I ceased to turn within to him who, so obscurely, so hiddenly, drew me to himself. Without this special grace I could not have gone to him.
—*BLG*, 33–35

I had imbibed an image of what was expected of a Carmelite.

She should be aflame with love for God. I was stone cold.

She should want suffering and be good at bearing it. I shunned it and was bad at bearing it.

No angry, resentful, envious, mean, competitive thoughts and impulses should sully a mind and heart given to God. I had all these things in abundance.

A Carmelite loved all the observances of the life. I found most of them boring and some made me angry as I felt they impinged on my dignity.

A Carmelite loved nothing better than solitude, to be alone with God alone. I wanted love, interest, variety; I wanted lots of things!

In short, I felt I was a sham, pretending to be something I was not. I lacked a natural religious sense and feared I was an agnostic if not an atheist at heart.   —*LU*, 3–4

[M]y whole being seems poised to leap toward another person. Ideas, things, cannot really touch me. They occupy and amuse me a little but fail to touch *me*. This "me" is experienced as an incompleteness, as a half-thing meaningless in itself and bleeding, moaning, groaning, tormented until it finds its other self, until it is united to another person. Here, undoubtedly, is a strong sexuality. This human need which, in God's plan, is normally orientated to marriage, the symbol-fulfillment, in its profoundest reality is a need for God and, in my own case, this was experienced without mitigation. The sheer exposure of Carmel, the absence of distraction, sharpened its edges intolerably. By the grace he gave me at the moment of conversion, he had, so to speak, "killed" creatures for me. He knew well with what hungry passion I would fall on them only to find them cheats, but not before I had ruined them and myself. No ideas of God could touch me. I wanted him, the living God, wanted him to be bound to my inmost self, to be one with him—I knew not how—but there must be no "separation," no "space" between. Lovely thoughts, those acts of faith and love, remained "outside" me, mysteriously deepening the sense of loss, absence. "This is for others, not for me. Others can drink of this fountain but it is barred to me. He is the God of others, he loves them, they please him, are dear to him, but I am outcast, cut off from him. He cares nothing for me."

Indeed, had I any real assurance that he existed? Life, and my dim experience of it, was just too deep, baffling, and suffering to be enclosed in glib words and concepts. I am not including the beloved figure of the gospels in that last phrase. God forbid! I hung on his words. It was his God I believed in. He had lived a human life, gone through it all, gone through death and then told us to have confidence. It was true, all would be well. "Fear not." And so I lived by these assurances, tried to live as if I believed and loved, but icy, fearful hands forever clutched and tore at my heart. How can I describe it? Jesus, too, was outside me. In my catechism I had learned that he was in heaven and in the Blessed Sacrament—not everywhere, not "in" me.

—*BLG*, 79–80

It is impossible to understand my life unless it is seen all the time against the background of black depression. This was my atmosphere. It was only a matter of degrees. It was like a blight and I could not understand it. In those days we did not think in terms of temperament or psychology. I concluded that there must be something wrong with my spiritual life. I had had no training.

There was no one to teach me how to pray. If only someone would come along who knew both the way to God and my own heart. . . .

The heart of this depression seems to have been fear, fear not of this or that precisely, but an ultimate fear, fear of my relation to God. Unless one has security in the Absolute; unless there is ground to being and ground to my own being then any assurances, any "security," is mockery. To enjoy anything is mockery. A condemned man faced with a good meal! How acutely I felt all this. Life seemed to be poisoned. Yet, given the fact of God and his revelation, what I was thinking and feeling was sin, displeasing to him . . . Oh there was no way out. No way except complete trust, dropping below this immense misery into the mercy of God. Gradually, in the fine point of my being, I was beginning to do this.   —*BLG*, 80–81

The year before my final profession, James married and brought his bride to see me on the evening of the wedding. I was deeply moved to see him so changed, to see their radiant happiness. I thought of them going off together, to the intimacy of their first night. No sooner had they left the parlor than I burst into a fit of weeping. My own lot seemed utterly bitter. Nothing, nothing, nothing, bleak, cheerless, lonely. And yet I found myself turning in the darkness to him, telling him I would go on to the end of my days feeling loveless if it pleased him. Truly there was a citadel within held by the living God.

Often the image would spring to my mind of myself in a little boat without oar or sail, on the vast expanse of ocean beneath a midnight sky. There was a sense of terror at the loneliness, at the dreadful depth below, at the utter helplessness of my state, but also the glorious security, unfelt though it was, of being held and controlled by the unseen God. I knew that I would rather be in that little boat with "nothing" than enjoy all that the world could offer me. I was wrapped around, clasped in mystery.
                                                   —*BLG*, 82–83

SURRENDER IN TRUST

The selections in this section show Rachel (or "Petra" in the passage from Guidelines for Mystical Prayer) *growing to accept her poverty as a gift. Aided by her stubborn meditation on the Gospels, the writings of St. Thérèse of Lisieux, and some theological works, Rachel realized that her bleak, unsatisfactory state is the ground from which the kenotic Jesus stands empty-handed before the Father's ecstatic love. She must thus surrender her nothingness to God in trust; there is no other mystical secret.*

At the end of her life St. Thérèse [of Lisieux] declared that she "had understood humility of heart." Here I am daring to say that I too have understood humility of heart. I do not say that I am humble of heart but I understand that the principal work of God is to bring us to true humility and poverty of spirit, to make us deeply aware of our nothingness so that he can give himself to us. Everything depends on our willingness to stand in the truth, to refuse to escape from this painful revelation of self, to accept to stand naked before the living God. At this time I was far from grounded in trust, that trust which casts itself into the arms of God, but I was growing toward it. After a fall, after some revelation of my weakness, feeling utterly wretched, when my instinct was to sulk spiritually, or at least be sluggish (through disgust with myself) in returning to God with full heart, recalling the story of the prodigal and that the father had embraced him in his smelly rags and that it was the father who cleansed and adorned him, I would say to him: "I ask you to love me all the more, to do more and more for me just because I have failed." This quiet inward working, this gentle turning to God in rain, fog, sleet, has gone on unremittingly. Although I might express in words bitterness, despair, utter frustration, my heart spoke lovingly to God. Often I would be gripped in emotional rebellion and resentment—but my heart would lie in suffering acceptance at God's feet.   —*BLG*, 73–74

It was not only this sense of being hopeless when it came to
praying that worried me. I seemed to have just the same bad
propensities as when I entered. I was ambitious. I wanted to
be Number One always. My thoughts were often critical and
unkind. Such things were incompatible with progress in the spiritual life, I thought. As far as I was aware, there was not a spark
of love for God in my heart. I was weary and sick of spiritual
things.

This general state of helplessness, the anxieties and fears that
beset me, found an answer in humility and trust. "Humility is
the ointment for all our wounds," says St. Teresa [of Avila]. God
would never spurn a contrite and humble heart. "Ask and you
will receive"; "With God all things are possible"; "How can a
man raise himself to Thee for he is born and bred in misery,
unless Thou raise him up with the hands that made him." These
are the words with which I sustained myself. They were a reality
to me.

In my distress, at every revelation of my sinfulness and weakness I would fall back into this humility and trust and find peace.
However, I saw this only as a provisional state, a sort of substitute until God gave me the real thing, so to speak. It was either
this or despair. It was not a way I chose. I was driven to it as a
last resort. Given the choice, no doubt I would have preferred
a more interesting and satisfying spiritual life. This is where
Thérèse [of Lisieux] came in and illumined my way for me.

The letters I refer to form part of the Autobiography but in
their original form they are more moving and powerful. Thérèse
is responding to her eldest sister's request for some thoughts of
her heart, and exposition of her doctrine. Using the metaphor of
a bird longing to fly to the sun but unable to do so because of its
utter weakness, she describes her attitude of daring, unshakeable
trust. . . . I was reading about my own self. . . .

By the grace of God I was able to take Thérèse literally. I
knew that what she said was pure truth. What is more, I was
that soul so much weaker than herself and I turned with trust

to God as she said. He has answered my trust and will answer it still more. . . .

Oh Thérèse, I have understood. All my being understands. Poverty of spirit . . . This is God's grace in me. —*MS*

As a young Carmelite, I was constantly exposed to the Liturgy. I studied the prayers of the Mass and the texts of the Divine Office throughout the liturgical year. The only form of "piety" that made any appeal to me was what I would now call biblical theology. I read and reread the Gospels; prayed and prayed the stories and dialogues, seeing myself always as the person Jesus was confronting, and begging Jesus for the same graces of cleansing and healing: for sight, living water, food, faith, love . . . I also prayed his own prayers: in the course of his ministry, at the last supper and in the garden, and, of course, these prayers were to the Father. Often, I used to think of those nights he spent alone praying to his Father, and wanted to identify myself with this prayer. I did all this as the most obvious response to what I was being shown and offered in the Gospel. I found similar incentives to pray in the words of Paul, John, and others, turning their magnificent statements of theology into personal prayers; and I would beg with all my heart for the fulfillment in me of what these wonderful texts were revealing concerning God's incredible designs of love. . . . The New Testament became prayer. I realized that God spoke to me, revealed himself to me in these texts, and my prayer was my response.

In this way, almost unconsciously, my prayer took a Trinitarian form. I knew that the lodestone of my being, inaccessible, utterly beyond the range of thought or feeling, had come to us and looked at us in pure friendliness and love through the eyes of Jesus. In Jesus the Inaccessible was accessible and very intimate, dwelling within. There was no need to climb to heaven, no need to strive for illumination. Useless, anyway. Through looking at Jesus, praying and trying to live the Gospel, I came to realize that the Inaccessible is absolute Love, and nothing but love. Love has come to us, is with us. God is not just "God" but God is always "God-with-us," "God-for-us," "God-who-has-us" in his heart.

—*EP*, 58–60

An objective, theological help to prayer came with my finding a passage in *The Lord* by [Romano] Guardini. I was thrilled when I read these words: "For the glorified Christ no limitations exist—also none of person. He can inhabit the believer, not only so that he constantly thinks of Christ or loves Him, but actually, as the human soul inhabits the body. Body and soul, Christ can inhabit the believer, for God's Son is not only soul, Spirit, but holy, glorious Reality, mystical Corpus. As such He is the renewer of life."

This was the first time I had met this thought. Hitherto I had learned that "Christ dwelt by faith in your heart" meant he dwelt in us merely through our thinking of him and loving him. He dwelt in us as Word but not as man. How puzzling! The Word is man forever.

Again, "The Spirit of God opens all things, permitting being to flow into being, life into life, me into you without violence or loss of individuality." This was the sort of thing I was looking for. I could now commune with Jesus "within me." . . .

At this time, I read Karl Adam's *Christ of Faith*. . . . It brought me definitive light. He discusses the Thomistic and Scotist views on person and nature and shows how these affect the understanding of Our Lord's human experience. Adam comes out on the side of Scotus in this argument. He goes on to suggest Our Lord's human experience. All my being cried out, "This is truth." How moved I was! Here was a theologian supporting my longings.

Our Lord knew the sense of absence from God. His was an utterly true humanity. I shall never forget the impact of his paragraph on the Incarnation and kenosis, the Word's stepping over the boundary into creation, leaving behind him all his prerogatives, coming into the world utterly defenseless, at our mercy.

A little later I read [F. X.] Durrwell's *Resurrection* and found the same rich teaching there. He speaks of the "weakness of this impoverished life of Jesus," the basic abasement of the Sacred Humanity in the days of his flesh. "Truly He shared our existence according to the flesh. Not in appearance only was He a slave: His subjection was rooted in nature. His earthly existence did not express His deepest reality . . . the secret glory of His holiness was locked in the depths of His being . . . Not only in His body, but all the faculties, even intellectual, by which He was in contact with the world and through which He carried out our redemption, were so incompletely possessed by the divine life that He was able to experience in them the need of being comforted by God."

I was to feed on this doctrine. It was to nourish my understanding of poverty. How foolish to wish to feel sublime when Jesus accepted such poverty and gave himself to his Father in it. Always he was the beloved of the Father. In this life we share his lowly state. In heaven we shall share his glory. This lowly state is really a sharing in his glory. It seems to me, in praying the invocation of the offertory of the Mass, that we may share the divinity of him who deigned to share our humanity, we are really praying to share to the full his humanity, for the grace to accept to be fully human, to taste the salt dregs of humanness as he did and to offer to the Father the pure selfless heart of his Son crying to him from our earth.   —*MS*

Having determined to give my life to prayer in the deepest meaning of that word, my expectations, vague though they were, were utterly shattered. I had no ability to pray; God remained utterly remote to me at the level of conscious experience. I had no sense of his presence, of being enfolded in love. Did I have any faith, I would ask myself. I could not claim that I had, that I could love either my neighbor or God if left to myself. If I had relied only on my merely human perception, how I felt things to be, I would have despaired and given up, telling myself it was all a great confidence trick! Or, if not that, then, at the least, that I myself was an abject failure and it was of no use to go on trying. But I didn't rely on myself; I took Jesus very seriously.

I saw that my total helplessness was expressing a fundamental truth: we cannot save ourselves, cannot attain God, cannot cope with God, still less show off in his presence. To the bewildered disciples' question: "Who then can be saved?" Jesus answered: "It is impossible for humans but not for God. For everything is possible to God" (Mark 10:27). Now I was experiencing this truth for myself. God has given us Jesus to be, as Paul tells us, "our wisdom, our unhindered access to God, our holiness and our atonement" (1 Cor. 1:30). So it doesn't matter when we feel our faith is very weak, hardly exists, or that we do not see, can't make sense of things: Jesus sees, Jesus knows and we are in Jesus. "Christ is mine and all for me" says St. John of the Cross. He is my wisdom, my faith, and his love is mine to love with. So we can afford to live with our poverty and, when we do so, it means that Jesus is *really* our only savior—which is what he is for. I don't want the impossible task of saving myself, of producing, from any supposed resources of my own, a faith that moves mountains. I have come to understand that God has done it all for us in giving us Jesus. Our part is to *use* him to the uttermost. . . . Identified with Jesus, we can afford to be very small, like "little children" and, just like a confident, cherished child, we can take it for granted that our Father will do everything for us.
—*EP*, 60–62

In one of my first interviews with Fr. Bernard, I was saying something to the effect that I had been given, for one brief moment, a glimpse of the mountain top, veiled indeed, but a glimpse nevertheless—referring to the dark, powerful illumination of my seventeenth year. "And you are still climbing the mountain?" he queried. To which I made the surprising reply, "In a way, I have got there." . . . What I said sprang from my heart without reflection. I was to make a similar statement later and again recently. Each time I meant the same thing but with, I hope, deeper reality. What did I mean? I was referring to that profound surrender in trust; the surrender of poverty to God. I realized then, as I realize even more now, that this gave me to God and God to me.

This was the essence of union, of sanctity. Not for a moment did I think I was perfect. Perfection has nothing to do with it. Given this profound hand-over, nothing can keep one from God. I expect to be imperfect to the end of my life and yet I am certain that God will accomplish in me all that he wills. It is the certainty that nothing can separate us from the love of Christ . . . that Power finds its full scope in weakness . . . that we are created and predestined by a God of love who seeks only to give himself to us. This was the rock on which my life was based. Usually it was submerged by the furious waves and I could not perceive it. I was conscious only of the darkness and the storm but, given the impulse, I could test its presence.   —*BLG*, 112

Fundamental to me is a natural fragility. My whole make-up inevitably, I think, must experience void, peril, aloneness. Only an extraordinary mystical grace could cancel these negative experiences, and God has not chosen to give me this and I do not expect that he ever will. He gave me one to "start me off," to awaken me to seek for him, to give my whole self to him, to show me that he alone was the meaning of existence. For the rest, it is his will that I should grope painfully along, experiencing to the depths what it is to be human, a frail, human creature, belonging with all her fibers to this world yet summoned beyond it, to a destiny bound up with the living God; a child of earth called to be, dare I say it, the Son of God, for this is what it means to be a Christian, to be taken up into Jesus, to be identified with him, to become son in the Son; to enter the very family life of the Trinity. "He became poor that we might become rich." I was to experience the bare bones of human poverty.
      —*BLG*, 55

For years I worried so. From all I read it seemed taken for granted that unless one received mystical graces then one was a second-class citizen with a second-class ticket. I was quite sure I'd received no mystical graces; I was dry as a bone and always had been. It wasn't that I coveted the experience I read about; on the contrary it put me off, but that sort of experience seemed a hallmark of God's favor and confirmed that one was pleasing to him. Later on common-sense came to my rescue, common-sense and faith. God is good, is faithful. If I trust him and surrender to him in whatever way I see, then I need have no worries; somehow I began to suspect that the answer was that somewhere along the line was a big mistake, a big misunderstanding; I sought to find it.

I was not left to search alone. God sent Claire to me. I had been told her way of prayer was extraordinary, that in fact she was a mystic. I had become skeptical by now . . . having come up a lot against what was classed as mystical. So up went my antennae and, to change the metaphor, I sniffed her suspiciously from head to foot. My skepticism was disarmed, my prejudice destroyed. "There is nothing pseudo here," I thought, "every note rings true. Here is profound humility and total surrender to God. Only God matters to this woman. She is immersed in God. Jesus lives in her." Long association has in no way lessened but only confirmed this opinion. I have no hesitation in calling Claire a mystic. . . .

It was Claire who drew my attention to Petra. I had known her for many years and certainly she was a faithful nun but there was nothing to single her out. In some ways others seemed more generous and sacrificial. She did nothing more than what others were doing. Claire told me quite emphatically that Petra was a mystic. I asked her why she said that. What did she see in Petra? "Petra never says 'no' to God, is always looking to him to see what he wants and, chief of all, accepts to be totally poor, to have no holiness of her own." Oh, what an answer to my search this was! If this ordinary woman, who like me had never known spiritual experiences, who was always in darkness and aridity, was a true mystic just as Claire was, then mysticism had nothing to do with "experiences." What was mysticism? Surely Jesus living in one, self drained away. I began to question Petra and she admitted simply that she knew Claire was right. She was aware, in a way that she could not explain, that she was closely united to God, that she no longer lived her own life.   —*GMP*, 2–3

THE ONLY WAY

Rachel writes because the heart of her story is the heart of everyone's story. No matter what security our temperaments may or may not afford us, in the end, we can only go to God with empty-handed trust.

My purpose in being autobiographical is simply to tell you how I came to have an indestructible conviction that the weaker, the more wretched and poor we are, the more we realize that we have no goodness of our own, and cleave to Jesus with might and main, taking him absolutely at his word that he has come to save sinners, that he has come as our servant, our healer, the more is he able to do everything for us.   —*LU*, 4

I could not—and cannot—follow what seems the classical spiritual journey. God does not ask it of me. He has provided another way for me. It may appear a poor sort of way, even a cowardly one, but it is my way and his choice for me. More than that, I know that, ultimately, in its essence, it is the only way. Sooner or later everyone must be brought by him to this deep poverty, and everything depends on acceptance of it. Personalities, temperaments differ and God leads all according to their own character. Roads may appear different but ultimately they converge. Sooner or later we must take the narrow path and leave behind all our spiritual riches. We have to go to God with empty hands. We have to let him be wholly and totally God. How hard this is. We want to feel good, want to feel we have something to offer him of our own. We want to be spiritually beautiful, to have an interesting, beautiful spiritual life. In his mercy he deprived me of all from the beginning. He has kept me in a state of poverty and helplessness. Now he has given me the grace to want this, to choose it.

St. Thérèse [of Lisieux] was to say that the suffering face of
Jesus was the heart of her spirituality. A fact rarely alluded to. I
can say the same. I have come to realize that the mystery of my
own life lies here. From the first he has hidden his face from me,
his face of glory. He has revealed his suffering, humbled face, the
man of sorrows who came to sit with us in our loneliness, in our
absence from God, in our desolation and wretchedness, in our
hunger and thirst. He drank the salt dregs of humanness and has
asked me to share it with him.   —*BLG*, 114–15

If I were to say that what I want to show people is that what
really matters is utter trust in God; that this trust cannot be there
until we have lost all self-trust and are rooted in poverty; that
we must be willing to go to God with empty hands, and that the
whole meaning of our existence and the one consuming desire of
the heart of God is that we should let ourselves be loved, many
spiritual persons would smile at my naïveté. They are likely to
murmur: "But we know all that; we can read that in any spiritual book. Does she think she is telling us something new?" All
I can say is that, although I too have known this in theory, it is
only now that it is integrated into my life. At least, so it seems.
Probably in five years' time or even next year, I will realize that
now I know next to nothing about it. What is more, looking at
my dear friends, living for God, wanting only him, I see in fact
that something is yet wanting to them. They have not come to
perfect trust. They feel they are spiritual failures because this has
not happened to them and that has not happened to them; they
feel they have missed out on something because their experience
carries none of the features which treatises on prayer and the
contemplative life seem to demand as signs of a truly authentic
spiritual life. They know they are loved by God and are pleasing to him and yet there is an indefinable anxiety which inhib-
its that total surrender to love which bridges the gap between
the virtuous man or woman and the saint. It seems to me that
God is asking one thing more and only one thing more, and
this, precisely, is what they are refusing to give. It is, in fact,

the deepest self-denial and so different from the ways in which they are seeking to do things for God and, as it were, trying to wrest God's good pleasure from his reluctant heart. This refusal seems to me to spring from lack of insight and understanding, certainly not from lack of good will. I see these dear people, self-giving, generous to a degree, full of love for God and yet still anxious, still hesitant before the last step which will release them from themselves and bury them in God. I see them turning, with a sense of failure, to new ideas on prayer which might perhaps "work better" though this is certainly not the term they would use. Yoga, Zen, Pentecostalism—these may have something to offer. I long to convince them that there is no need for this, that here and now, in their present "unsatisfactory" state, in their "failure," God is giving himself to them; that this state of poverty is precisely what he wants and his way into them. He has labored with love to open up this way and will they now block it? I could tell them that, in fact, they are turning from the straight path up the mountain, the path of poverty, and choosing the winding road of spiritual riches.

I have known this doubt, this tearing anxiety to a frightful degree. For nearly thirty years I have groped in darkness. But to some extent, at any rate, now I see. In these days of sharing and dialogue, it cannot be thought out of place, pride and presumption, to want to share my insight with others. There is absolutely nothing extraordinary or "interesting" in my life. It is completely common-place. But it may be that the sheer commonplaceness will help others. I feel that it is in the story of my life, of my own search and journey, that what I want to say will be revealed and may strike home in a way that a purely theoretical exposition of these truths will never do.   —*BLG*, 2–3

Each of us has a unique vocation most likely conditioned by our natural temperament—or shall we say that our natural temperament mysteriously forms part of our vocation? My vocation is no more unique than that of anyone else and for all I know many people may feel as I do. However, it does seem to me that

I have been called to experience and accept human reality in a
sharp way. It is not an easy vocation but possibly it enables me
to discern rather clearly the naked structure of the human vocation which is, of course, the Christian vocation. My life in Carmel has aided and abetted this clarification for, as I understand
it, Carmel exists for the purpose of enabling persons to live at
great depth, naked before the living God.   —*LM*, 12–13

2

The Gift of God

How God loves us, how total is the divine self-gift to each one of us. —LM, 82

From this chapter onward, the selected passages draw out the various aspects of the Gospel wisdom embodied in the story of Rachel's life. We begin with the God revealed by Jesus. This is a God who is complete self-gift, a God of total outpoured love. Rachel writes with authority, as one who surely knows what she is talking about. Yet she asserts, "I have [had] nothing, ever, ever, never, on the level of what I could within myself feel, let's say, of God's love for me, God's presence to me. Never, I can honestly say that, never have I" (Interview, September 30, 2009). Clearly, this is a knowledge borne by faith, a knowledge that is deeper and more enduring than the changing weather patterns of the emotions.

We read in these selections of God yearning to break through all resistance and give the fullness of Godself to his creation. The intimacy initiated with the people of Israel culminates in the mystical presence of God within us, drawing us through the crucified Jesus into the life of the Trinity.

A MYSTERY THAT DRAWS NEAR TO US

These selections convey Rachel's understanding of the centuries-long interplay between God's utterly gratuitous self-gift and humankind's tendency to resist such divine vulnerability. She highlights that while humans have tried to contain God, or to create God in their own image, the mystery of infinite love is always beyond our controlling grasp.

Holy Mystery. That has become my chosen way of speaking of ultimate reality. To say "God" is already to introduce revelation. "God" is a relational term and that it can be used of the holy Mystery, that the holy Mystery offers to be our God, we know only through revelation. The world, of itself, does not reveal God. Even so, our God remains total Mystery, inaccessible to the created intellect, indefinable. To speak of absolute Being is to reduce that of which we speak to the level of something of which we have experience—being. "Mystery," I suggest, leaves our subject outside all categories, beyond the range of words and concepts, stretching to infinitude. At least, it seems to me, the best we can do is to refuse definition or description.

—*LM*, 7

If we are to know God it can only be because he chooses to reveal himself. Between him and us there is an unbridgeable gulf that we ourselves, of ourselves cannot cross. He is completely "other," transcendent mystery, yet a mystery that draws near to us and lovingly beckons. It is he who has made the bridge across the abyss; he has opened a door into his own eternal being, and that door is Jesus.

The "world," that does not and cannot know God is human pride and self-sufficiency, the enemy of the God that really is. This world chooses to stand on itself, in a way of existence within its own bounds and control, and refuses the invitation to be drawn beyond itself into God's holy being. It resists with murderous panic the mystery that is Love. The world wants power over its god, wants to grasp him in the tentacles of knowledge, wants a puppet controlled by its own dictates—and this world is in us all.

—*OF*, 30

Human beings have always been implicitly aware of the mysterious nature of reality and, with their religious beliefs and rites,
have tried to come to terms with it, gain some control over the
mystery, ensure its good will and ward off its awful power. The
Old Testament is the story of a people's effort to deal with mystery. We find in its pages almost every ploy that human beings
use to impose order on chaos, give meaning to what is meaningless and to control by knowledge. But over and over again these
efforts are defeated by reality which is not what they would like
it to be and refuses to fit into their patterns of thought. Even so,
this people had courage to believe in what we call revelation:
that the incalculable, the unutterable Mystery had in some way
"spoken" to them, had not left them defenseless and in total
ignorance.

Holy Mystery had revealed itself to be their own God who
made demands indeed, but who cared. By a series of mighty
deeds, they had been rescued from ignominious slavery, forged
into a people and given a land of their own. Their sense of elec-
tion gave them identity as a people, the "people God has chosen as his own." What was privilege and responsibility became
self-glorification, an indisputable claim over God, a reduction of
holy Mystery to a god, a human projection of sinful hearts. We
can perceive through the Bible the human propensity to "tame,"
make manageable the holy Mystery, whereby God is no longer
independent reality . . . and always there comes the reaction, the
corrective vision, the prophet's pen scouring through illusion,
asserting once again the uncontrollable, utterly free, holy Mystery.   —LM, 8–9

This primal theme runs through the Bible: our God is a giving,
communicating God. He calls into existence what is not and
calls into fuller existence what is. He calls the winds, the waves,
the stars. He gives himself to everything that is according to its
capacity to receive him, be it the grass and flowers of the field,
the poor worm, the kingly beast or man.   —ICE, 9

"From the beginning" our Creator and Lover has striven to communicate himself to human beings. Historical facts and present experience show that "in many and varied ways" (Heb. 1:1) unknown to us, something of the truth of God has been revealed throughout the world. Nevertheless, divine Wisdom, Word, Love, chose a particular people in which to abide in a special way so that through this chosen people, knowledge of him would spread to every race on earth: "All the ends of the earth would see the salvation of our God" (Ps. 98(97):3). The Bible records the "fate" of the divine Word seeking a home with the "children of men." . . .

The Creator Spirit, always at work in the world and in human hearts, never contravenes their innate structure but works from within; not doing for men and women what they can do for themselves. True to their nature, for human nature is naturally religious, the Hebrew people sought for their God, sought for the face that, although they knew it not, was seeking them. Alas, their myopic vision as often as not perceived a hideous caricature, wrathful, vindictive, jealous for its honor. Although the Lord was knocking at the door, looking through the lattice, his face alight with love, longing to be welcome (Song of Sol. 2:9), poor, self-concerned, frightened men and women, projecting on to him their fear, their hate and anger, shut their doors and lattices.

Inexplicable, destructive natural phenomena inevitably aroused fear in primitive people and, of course, they attributed them to some wrathful deity. Dreaded too was the cruelty of powerful, rapacious foes. What they were wanting was a warrior god who would gird on his buckler and shield, and raise his mighty sword arm to crush their enemies. Through their great leader, Moses, they had learned that a God had chosen them to be his own people and had rescued them from slavery. It is the same God, so they were told, who had been worshipped by their father Abraham and was now to be known as the God of Israel. They must be loyal to him, worship him alone and have nothing to do with other gods.

Not until the exile did monotheism take hold and the prophet of the exile, Second Isaiah, was the first to give it unequivocal expression. Chapters 40 to 43, especially, are a verbal elimination of nature gods and of polytheism in general. It is hard for us to appreciate how great a spiritual achievement this was in a culture totally polytheistic. Even so, people quickly drifted back into idolatry. Utterly dependent on their harvest, subject to frequent droughts and the danger of famine, they rushed back to their fertility rites hoping thereby to placate the gods that sent rain in season, ensured fertility of human and beast. They had no illusions about the morality of their gods. Pagan gods shared the vices of human and were basically self-seeking, caring nothing for their worshippers, and yet generations of ancestors had had nothing else to rely on. Conveniently, these gods, having no morals themselves, made no moral demands on their clients.

Unfamiliar, strange and seemingly ineffectual, Israel's God did not fit the pattern. As yet they could not know how deeply he cared and how vulnerable he was in his love. Love made stern demands that served their truest interest; to ignore them spelled disaster. However, to their way of thinking, the one supposed to be their God was shown to be powerless, unable—or unwilling—to take care of them. He did not go out with their armies to ensure their victory but let them be defeated!

He was indeed a hidden God. They saw the long, successful reign of David and Solomon as the golden age and blithely assumed that what God wanted for his people was what they wanted: a return of that golden age, when Israel would once again be a strong, independent people under its own king, taking its proud place among the nations. They were sadly mistaken. . . .

As revelation develops, we shall see this reversal of human values constantly repeated. In carrying out his inconceivably wonderful, blissful design for all humankind and the whole of creation, the Creator, from the quasi-infinitude of the cosmos, selects one tiny, insignificant planet to be a home of incredible beauty for his human creatures. When he comes to earth as one of us, he chooses for his earthly dwelling, not splendid Greece or Rome, but Palestine, a vulnerable coastal strip, and not its capital, Jerusalem, but Nazareth, an insignificant village, and the home of a little nobody, a virgin named Mary.

The Bible is a monumental drama of good and evil, light and darkness; every human passion is displayed and every human sin. Divine Love wandered unrecognized, unsheltered among the children of men, crying out: "Where are you?" (Gen. 3:9).

—*LU*, 52–56

THE GIFT OF GOD THAT IS JESUS CHRIST

The pattern of vulnerable divine love trying to break through and self-sufficient humanity refusing to accept the gift is finally overcome in Jesus. In these passages, Rachel sets before our eyes Jesus crucified, the human image of the mystery of divine love lavishing itself upon us. The Crucified is utterly transparent to God's self-emptying love, astounding us with the revelation of how absolutely God is given over to us.

Can we believe that God comes so close, is so bound up with us as this image reveals? See how, of the four connecting circles, the center one is the focus of the other three. Within that circle lies helpless "man." The divine Trinity comes down to his aid, the Father gently lifting him up and tenderly pressing his holy face against the leprous cheek; the Son kneels to kiss his dirty, crippled feet delighting in being his servant; as a dove in flames, the Spirit, mutual love of Father and Son, swoops down to complete "man's" enfolding into the unspeakable glory of the triune life.

This image powerfully summarizes the mystery of the Incarnation. Who could have dreamed that the Creator of the universe, too great for any created mind to comprehend (Isa. 40:12–26 & others), would choose to become defenseless as a slave, totally immersed in our feverish, sinful, suffering existence, yearning humbly for our love, prepared to expend himself to win it? So loved are we! So loved! Shall we be his joy and delight, or shall we break his heart?

Sr. M. Caritas Müller, OP, "The Merciful Trinity"

When we pore over the gospels, our heart in our eyes, longing to know our beloved Lord; as we watch him, listen to him we see more and more the true nature of our God, what our God is *really* like. God has revealed himself as pure compassion and love. —*QUD*, 1

In former times God used various ways to enlighten us but now he has spoken once for all by his Son. All other modes of communication are abolished. Formerly God could not make himself understood; there was no one of sufficient transparency to receive him. Now there is. Jesus is the definitive revelation of God; God has nothing more to reveal. You crave to know, be reassured, have a guarantee? Jesus will satisfy it. You look within at your own subjective feelings but what do they tell you? They can give no certitude. You have all the guarantee you need in Jesus. See what he has shown us of the Father's steadfast love, of his will to give us everything. See how he reveals the Father as total forgiveness. What need have you of further reassurance?

—*AL*, 97

[T]he New Testament proclaims—it is the good news it bears—that "God," however we might conceive of "God" (and inevitably the human heart, consciously or unconsciously, forms some idea of God to affirm or deny), can be known only through Jesus Christ and Jesus Christ as crucified. This is the revelation that stuns merely human wisdom and all those ideas of God that derive from the human mind and heart. It is the revelation of the divine that to the Jews was an obstacle they could not surmount, a scandal pure and simple, and to the pagans was ludicrous folly. Jesus of Nazareth, in his unprotected, raw human-ness, in his weak and suffering flesh and, supremely, in his terrible Passion and death, is clean contrary to human ideas of the divine (1 Cor. 1:22–4).

This may seem a startling affirmation. What about the Resurrection? Jesus' earthly life, his Passion and death, belong to the past. Surely it is the glorious, risen Christ with whom we have to do, and it is this glorious One who is the image of God? Undoubtedly. But what can we see of this Risen One? As Luke tells us clearly, the holy cloud of the divine Mystery took him from human sight (Acts 1:9). We know the heart of the Risen One, how he is to us, what he does for and in us, precisely through his earthly life and in his Passion and death. The Risen One, "at the right hand of the Father," is Jesus and none other. We know that within the very heart of the Trinity, in "heaven," there is that same passion of love for us, that same Self-expending outreach, that "nothing spared," that sheer excess of love which, in the reality of this world and ourselves as we are, found its most expressive form in the denuded, dispossessed man on the gibbet.

This is the Christian God, the living God, the God who really is. This is the God whom Jesus called Father, whose image he is, and who must be surrendered to or denied. What of ourselves? If we examine our ideas . . . do we not uncover assumptions regarding the Godhead that derive from human wisdom and that we have transposed onto Jesus and, from him, onto Jesus' God and Father? We can and perhaps do create a Jesus in the image and likeness of God but it is a God of our human conception. This will always be our natural tendency. We fail to know him even as the Jews of old failed to "see" Jesus or recognize who he is. Progressively, painfully, with many a backward slither, each and every one of Jesus' followers has to allow Jesus—his person, his life, his death, and his Resurrection—to correct, perhaps even to destroy and then reshape, their understanding of God. Theoretical knowledge is not enough. We suffer from the same inbuilt blindness and resistance to recognition as they did. Possibly it is Paul who expresses most dramatically this radical collapse of God, the God he had served with zeal and passion. We see him literally thrown to the ground and blinded by the vision—of what? . . . The crucified Jesus as the very wisdom and power of God! (Acts 9:1–9; 22:6–11; Gal. 1:15–16). Such a revelation can come only from God. Paul was sure of this; it was none other than God himself who revealed his Son. Such knowledge as this transcends human wisdom. It is "what eye has not seen, nor ear heard" (1 Cor. 2:9).

If we want to know God, Reality, Bedrock and Ground, Absolute Origin, ineffable Mystery, that in which we and all that is exist as tiny fish in an infinite ocean, we must look at Jesus crucified. Holding up the cross, bidding us gaze into that bleeding, humiliated face, the Holy Spirit's focus is not first and foremost on suffering, or even on sin and its consequences, but on a love that is absolute, "out of this world," "other," "what no eye has seen, nor ear heard, nor the human heart conceived." We must gaze and gaze with fullest attention and then affirm: this is God; this is what God is really like. Through this vision we have the certainty of what is beyond our comprehension, that God is love and nothing but love, and that he is love to and for us. It is not enough merely to affirm God's loving interest and care—one need not be a Christian to hold that sincerely. What we see in

Jesus is a Self-gift on God's part that is the fullest content of love. God gives not gifts but God's own Self. . . .

Any notion whatsoever that sets a figure of divine wrath over and against Jesus, who not only demands just retribution for human iniquity but demands it of Jesus in our stead, a Father who imposes an appalling sacrifice on the Son while he himself remains aloof, untouched, in the realms of the divine, can only be considered blasphemous by us today, whatever its pedagogical value to former generations. It is the Evangelist John who shows us clearly the communion of life, heart, and will between Father and Son. It is the Father's excess of love for us that, in filling the heart of Jesus, drives Jesus to his self-emptying. In keeping nothing back from us, loving us to the uttermost, giving us his all, we know that it is the Father living in him who is keeping nothing back from us and giving us his all. In giving us Jesus he gives us his all.   —*EP*, 44–47

Throughout the gospel narratives we see the incarnate Lord's predilection for what is lowly, in the world's estimation unimportant even worthless. The reputation of being a miracle-worker distressed him and he begged those whom he cured not to publicize the fact. Jesus was totally concerned with his Father's interests not at all with himself. He shunned praise: "Why do you ask me about what is good? One there is who is good" (Matt. 19:17). Unassuming, endlessly serviceable, abhorring ostentation, poor, gentle, self-expending, such was the human life of God.

The Incarnate Word's way of living confronts us with an awesome insight into the very nature of God. "God is love" (1 John 4:16) and God loves with a love of which our human love even at its purest and deepest is but a faint echo. True love is always humble, vulnerable, tremulously offering itself, incapable of force and freely exposed to hurt and rejection; rejected, "love lies bleeding." Love is self-gift and therefore self-emptying. Jesus' kenosis, his "ecstasy" of love for his Father and his Father's love for Jesus, "my Son and the delight of my heart" reveal that the Holy Trinity is a mystery of self-giving, ecstatic love, a selflessness that is the cause of all that is. We are made in the image of God and selfless love must be the heartbeat of our life also.   —*QUD*, 10

It is so difficult for us to grasp the reality of the Incarnation: the truth that our great God, our holy Creator, has, so we may say, thrown off his robes of grandeur and run out in eagerness to meet us, to be with us where we are. There are promises of this in the Old Testament: "I will dwell in your midst," "Emmanuel." It is simply too good to be true! It just can't be true! But it *is* true. . . .

We are saying that the Word, which is the self-expression of God and therefore God, actually *becomes* something other than he is, becomes a made thing, a creature. Put it another way, God becomes something he was not before, acquires a new form of existence, a new experience, namely, that of being human, flawed as we are, from conception to death, in this world as it is. . . .

Only God, while remaining God, can become something other. The "becomes" is absolute. God *becomes* man—no pretense, absolute reality.

And so we return to gaze upon this tiny, fragile helpless little creature, totally dependent on his mother for his coming into the world and for the preservation of his fragile life. Were she not to feed him, caress him, keep him warm, he would die. . . .

Why has the all-blessed One let himself in for this! What a crazy, crazy thing for him to do! Yes, it is and the only answer is that he is "crazy" in his love. . . .

From now on the Eternal God-become-man is completely in our hands, for us to do with him what we wish; we can treat him with love, with indifference or hatred. In his human nature he draws on no divine power, on no divine knowledge to defend himself from malice or to attain his end. He has "emptied" himself of his divine attributes; speaking metaphorically, he left them behind on the other side of the border. . . . He has come to be with us, to share our human existence, to heal and save us: "My people is stricken with a very grievous wound which only I can heal. True, they are wounded by the consequences of sin, but there is a deeper wound still, that only I can perceive and which they themselves scarcely recognize. It is a wound of love that I myself have inflicted, an open wound for which there is no natural healing. I myself *am* the healing of that wound, that ever-aching, unsatisfied desire." Could we conceive of any greater love than is shown us here—in this conception and birth? We know it is all one with that final surrender to a cruel death. . . .

. . . God himself, none other, comes down to us to be with us in the "pit" in order to take us up to "be with me where I am" (John 17:24) and for ever. God gives his entire Self, holding nothing back, nothing whatsoever. His love for us is absolute. It falls to us to fix our minds and hearts on the Gift of God that is Jesus Christ our Lord, to make him the lodestar of our lives.

—*LU*, 13, 89–92, 100

What we must try to grasp is that God gives God's self totally to us. God has not a hidden, private life to which we have no access. A couple might run an orphanage and devote themselves utterly to their charges, sparing themselves nothing in their love and care, finding happiness in their happiness. And yet, the door on the orphanage can close and the couple enjoy their own intimate family life with their own children, a life from which the orphans are excluded. Not so with God. We are in God's heart forever. There is no God but the God who has us in his heart and who shares divine life with us.   —*LU*, 31

God is forgiveness. . . . A total amnesty is declared, unconditional forgiveness. All the writers of the New Testament proclaim this, it is the substance of the good news. It is the expression of divine Love's coming to meet us in the reality of our sinfulness.

What must this assurance of amnesty have meant to the ancient peoples? Almost of necessity they were religious, acknowledging a power outside themselves, a power to be feared, to whom they were answerable. There was little to assure them that they were in a safe relationship with a deity; that they stood blameless before it. Even the Jews were not exempt from this anxiety, as Paul, an observant Jew himself, so poignantly expresses. Their very law and the demands it made on them only highlighted their sinfulness and their inability to keep the law. It is clear that Paul is not referring merely to the externals of the Torah but its inner demands. He found himself helpless and he suffered a conflict between his natural selfishness and the light afforded to his spiritual self by the Torah. He was to describe himself as the greatest of sinners because he persecuted the Church. Paul was quite, quite sure that Jew as well as pagan stood before God as transgressors. Then in Jesus comes the incredible news, God does away with sin; it is alright, absolutely alright! God reconciles you to God! What you cannot do God does in glad, costly love. God takes the burden. . . .

. . . Jesus was listening to the Father, looking at him, and inevitably all that Jesus thought, said, did, mirrored, embodied how God is to us. . . . Jesus saw his Father as forgiveness. There was never a time when God was not forgiveness. God does not become forgiveness through any act of ours. Our repentance can only mean one thing, that we open our heart to the welcoming love of the Father. . . .

How often in the name of God, who is no true god, we lay intolerable burdens on others, even on little children. Instead of concentrating on showing them in one way and another, the tenderness, the compassion, the sheer friendliness of God, we warn about sin and its consequences, insist on rules and regulations, and hearts turn away from such a god. The human heart refuses to take such a god seriously or else "serves" God in fear, keeping every rule, clinging desperately to law and structures. If only each one of us would go to Jesus for a true picture of God! If only we prayed constantly: Let me see your face, let me hear your voice, for your voice is sweet, and your face is comely (Song of Sol. 2:14).

Luke gives us a cluster of revealing stories. Jesus is scandalizing the scribes and Pharisees by keeping company and eating with tax collectors and "sinners," people excluded from the

religious community. Jesus, a devout, observant Jew was doing
the unthinkable and certainly the non-acceptable. He was violat-
ing the boundaries between those acceptable to God because of
their obedience to the law, and those who, breaking these laws,
had set themselves "outside the mercy." There is no doubt that
the parables addressed an historical situation but the underlying
outlook and attitudes of those involved are universal and touch
the deep center of true religion and Jesus' message. As always,
the all-important focus of the parables is God, what God is like,
how God views us. . . .

The shepherd, full of concern for the strayed sheep, taking
it upon himself to look for it and bring it home; the housewife,
searching for her precious coin and sweeping diligently until she
finds it; the father of the prodigal running out to meet his home-
coming son, and the joy in finding; all three characters tell us of
God, of how God runs out to meet us, labors to find us, obliv-
ious of the grief we have caused. We are shown how precious
we are, what joy God has in us when we are at home, safe and
trusting in love. The sheep, the coin, contribute nothing to their
rescue and the prodigal's movement is minimal. It is the father
who brings him home, in distinction to his just being around the
place where he can eat, find shelter and survive. God is forgiveness. We have only to receive. No act of ours is needed to bring
a change in the divine heart to induce it to turn to us in mercy.

—*LM*, 61–63, 65–66

In John's account of the [last] supper, the first thing Jesus does
is kneel as a slave to wash the feet of his disciples: "I am among
you as a servant." Jesus is God! God our servant! . . . Such a
word as this, striking an open heart shatters it to pieces. Do we
know God at all?, I ask myself. There is only one way in which
we can truly know him and that is through Jesus, his perfect
image. Jesus' foot washing is a gesture of total self-giving, of
loving to the utmost; it has the same significance as the gift of
his immolated self under the symbols of bread and wine. In the
presence of the friend turned traitor who, at this very moment,

is intent on handing him over to his enemies, Jesus hands himself over completely to us in accordance with his Father's will. . . .

Many years ago, I came across a little French parable that moved me deeply, a parable of unbreakable sacrificial love. A widowed mother had an only son whom she cherished. Her tireless loving care was repaid with ingratitude. Heartless wretch that he was, heedless of her needs, time and again he left her, only to return when his pockets were empty and he was hungry. Each time, she would welcome him and supply his needs at cost to herself. Eventually, his selfish greed had stripped her of everything she had. On his return and finding her unable to give him what he wanted, he was furious and in anger tore her heart from her breast and in sheer contempt threw it on the ground. As he ran to the door, he fell over the heart, and the heart said: "Have you hurt yourself, my son?"   —*LU*, 130, 135

God in God's essence is totally unknowable. Yes. But I know that this same Mystery can be "known" and that the answer to all our yearning, our questioning, the fulfillment of our transcendence, is utterly close, intimate, available, not to thought or to emotion but to love. The "unattainable" is not a closed door but a welcome, a heart wide open to receive us. Through Jesus I know that the holy Mystery is not something but someone, not merely fullness of being but also and primarily fullness of love, a holy communion opening itself outwards to embrace all persons, gathering all home to itself.

I believe it is the Christian vocation, through its faith in Jesus, not merely to cut deeply through life's waters but to abandon ship, so to speak, and surrender fully to Mystery. It is a vocation and vocation calls for a life-long commitment in a surrender to the divine action we call grace. It is possible simply because we are loved.

With all the passion of my heart I declare Jesus, the crucified and risen one, to be the alpha and omega of all things, the first-born of creation, the holy Mystery's self-communication, the definitive Word of how and what that Mystery is to us. . . .

As Christians we hold only one certainty: God's unconditional love. But we live in space and time, in history, responding
to reality in its manifold forms. If the pure, white light is to be
loved by us and if we are to choose it of our own free will as our
true home, it must pass through a prism and be broken up into
different colors, not to deceive or decoy us but to increase our
yearning for the source of its beauty. In Catholic piety we speak
of the mysteries of Jesus' life on which we are invited to meditate. The liturgical season revolves around them: Jesus' birth,
his presentation in the Temple, his temptations in the desert, his
passion, death, and resurrection. Contemplation of each of these
separate mysteries opens us more profoundly to the one holy
Mystery of which these are reflections. If we look into dogmas,
try to understand what the Church means by them, we shall
perceive that these too are ways in which the love of God for us
is revealed.

For example, take the Marian dogmas of the Immaculate
Conception and Assumption. These, to some people, can seem
extraneous to the holy Mystery, pious wishful thinking which
has no right to be deemed certainty. What, in fact, we find in
both dogmas is a revelation of the holy Mystery's loving purpose for humankind. In this one woman we see the mystery of
what it means to say that we are chosen in Christ: "before the
foundation of the world, that we should be holy and blameless
before him" (Eph. 1:4). And for those whom he foreknew he
also predestined to be conformed to the image of his Son: "And
those whom he predestined he also called; and those whom he
called he also justified; and those whom he justified he also glorified" (Rom. 8:30).

Each of us may take these words to ourselves. Each of us, if
we choose to receive the grace offered, can cry with Mary that
the Lord has clothed us head to foot in his salvation, thrown
around us the cloak of his love, and made us holy (cf. Isa. 61:10).

Again, a careful examination of the dogma of purgatory
would yield further insight into the Mystery of love that is both
purifying and transforming.

Everything that the Church holds and teaches as truth is an elaboration of the one truth, a human attempt, under the guidance of the Holy Spirit, to draw out its implications so that it becomes the supreme reality of our lives. Inevitably, human weakness can obscure the truth. What is perfectly intelligible in one culture may be unintelligible in another; but sooner or later, again under the Spirit's guidance, this will be corrected as we have many times seen. Christianity when it is really true to itself, brings us to the point of obedient surrender—call it faith, call it love, when, rejecting every other security, we cast ourselves into the divine abyss, or stand exposed to unfiltered light. . . .

. . . [T]he infinite Mystery, the all "behind which there is nothing and before which there is nothing" offers its very self to us as our completion and total happiness. God's love, then, means God's unreserved self-donation to us, and our receiving this, becoming filled with the fullness of God, is the only possible human fulfillment. What follows is the guarantee that, if we accept, ultimately, "not a hair of your head will perish" our personal existence is affirmed, loved into total happiness. God's love can be utterly relied on to bring us this final bliss; nothing whatever can prevent it except our own choice, and everything we need will be at hand. Whatever it seems like we are not tossed around by fate. Each of us is a history of salvation being written by God. As our final end is beyond our grasp so are the mysterious workings of divine love to achieve this end. We are called to trust in the love that is totally devoted to us and can be relied on absolutely; that this holy Mystery, this indestructible horizon is pure, nurturing love I know only through Jesus. Without him, I, most certainly, could not know it.   —*LM*, 14–16, 18–19

Our idea of prayer will depend on the idea we have of God. We may see God as a distant, almighty, though benevolent being, to whom we must in duty bound offer our worship, thanksgiving, and petitions, coming before his throne at fixed times to acknowledge his rights over us and to pay him his dues. The rest of the time we get on with the business of living here on earth.

We know he is looking on, ready to reward our good actions and reprove us for our bad. The reward consists of a credit mark against our name in heaven and the sum total of these credit marks will decide the degree of glory and happiness in heaven when we die. Or we may understand that as a reward for our good acts, God gives us "grace," a mysterious something that makes us strong and beautiful and pleasing to him. The more filled with grace we are when we die, the happier we shall be in heaven. This is a caricature, no doubt, but possibly it comes nearer to the truth of our attitudes than we might care to admit.

In this context, prayer is a function in life and has very little to do with the rest of life. It ensures keeping on the good side of God. The truth is very different, and we learn the truth not from our poor, sinful hearts but from the revelation of Jesus. The teaching of the New Testament shows us God, not "out there" but most intimately present in the very heart and blood pulse of our lives. What is more, he is not a great lord who takes delight in the homage of his vassals and servants and is affronted when these are denied; he isn't interested in himself and his own advantage, he is only concerned with us and our happiness, and this happiness is his happiness. He is obsessed with us, wholly absorbed with caring for us; every detail of our lives, every cell of our body is a matter for his concern—our Lord tells us so. He has all the passionate, intense concern of the most loving of parents. Specifically, his one aim is to give us himself. This, as a simple statement, can mean little to us. We have to take it on faith that this is the highest, ultimate blessedness and until it is accomplished we remain unhappy, unfinished beings.

God is always wanting to come closer to us, and in his eyes the whole of our span of mortal life is meant to make us accustomed to his nearness. God loves us and love is always humble and respectful; it will not force itself upon the beloved. God cannot love us to the full, that is, give full scope to his love, be as lavish with us as he wishes, unless we let him. If, from his side, our lives in this world are an opportunity for him gradually to give himself until we are capable of receiving him fully, from our side they must be seen as a response to his loving advances, allowing him to train and fit us. There is never any question of the initiative lying with us or of our having to get on the good side of God in order to win his favors.   —*TBJ*, 78–79

DRAWN INTO GOD'S OWN RADIANT LIFE

If we are to participate in the dance of God's utter self-giving and complete human openness to this gift, we must be taken in in Jesus. In Rachel's thought, our becoming completely transparent to God's outpoured love through being transformed into Jesus is what is meant by the mystical life.

God, in his love, offers himself to us as our fulfillment and perfect happiness. He chooses to draw us into his own radiant life. He calls us to transcend our natural limitations. This call, his gracious working in us beyond our natural limits and operations, and the transcendent goal to be reached, are precisely what we call mystical. It is the old, familiar doctrine of sanctifying grace and the divine indwelling.   —*GMP*, 9

In the scriptures God is "holy" and this term was used in an effort to express his transcendence, his inmost being, his own world utterly separate from the world of men. It means God's own, unutterable existence. A human being is holy insofar as he has come into contact with divine holiness. For this, the divine holiness must have drawn near and touched him, for man, of himself, cannot enter the divine ambience. God's life is inaccessible to him. To be holy in the absolute sense means that a human being has been taken right into this ambience, that he lives with God, in God's own sphere. The writers of the New Testament speak of Christians as God's holy people; they are the saints, the holy ones. This means they are so in calling; the whole meaning of their vocation as Christians is to be drawn into the inmost heart of God. They are drawn in in Jesus who has made them his own. It is he, of humankind, who is the holy one absolutely, for he belongs completely to God; besides being on our side he

is also fully on God's side. By our union with Jesus we too can
enter, and do enter into God's holy world.

Holy in principle we have to become so in reality, we have to
allow God to come close to us and by his closeness make us like
him and able to live wholly in his sphere, his "eternal life." The
divine initiative cannot be overstressed. Too easily we think of
holiness as something we acquire. We do not acquire it but we
must labor to prepare for God's coming to us and work with
him when he draws near.   —*TBJ*, 90–91

I believe that a living grasp of Jesus' meaning—and that means
one that influences our whole life—is properly a mystical grace,
something the Holy Spirit must work in us. No amount of thinking about it, no conceptual knowledge can elicit it. But what we
can do is ponder over and over again the reality of God's freely
given love, as Jesus shows it to us, try to base our lives on this
love, hold firmly to the truth that we are in the Father's house,
already loved with no need to prove ourselves, no need to merit
an entrance into that hearth, home, and heart. It is all ours by
gift.

What is asked of us is that we should live as a loved child lives,
doing always what pleases the parent. In this way we can give up
the anxious fretting to be sure—sure that we are doing "right,"
that our motives are pure, and so forth. We cannot know these
things and there is no need to know. Rather, it is best that we do
not know. If we had the surety we crave, we would be relying
on ourselves, not leaning totally on the freely-given love of God.
                                                    —*LM*, 77–78

The Holy Spirit, the divine Energy of the love of the Father for
Jesus and of Jesus for his Father, will become divine Energy in us,
transforming our minds and hearts into what we behold—not
necessarily, and not most importantly, with our conscious mind,
but in the secret region where is our true life and identity. We
have to entrust ourselves in blindness and helplessness to divine
Love. The seed God sows is God's own life; it holds within itself

divine dynamism. How can it fail to grow if it falls into welcoming soil? The farmer, Jesus points out in another parable, is content to sow the seed and then wait patiently; there is nothing more that he can do. But, sure enough, there it is—the blade, the ear, the sheaf, the harvest home! —*LM*, 60

3

Created for the Gift of God

Our pride urges us to escape as much as we can from whatever forces upon us our fundamental state of dependency and helplessness; love for Jesus will make us understand and embrace it and in it find freedom.

—QUD, 33

This chapter is the complement of the preceding one. Here, Rachel explores with us the wonder that if God gives himself to each person in outpoured love, then to be human is to be created to receive this supreme gift. The sheer fragility of the human condition—which we each taste, in greater or lesser measure—is a reminder of our divine origin and destiny: we have been made as an emptiness only God can fill. For Rachel, we become fully human to the extent that we refuse to shield ourselves with the defenses presented by the ego and instead use the opportunities for "unselfing" presented by daily life to stand in empty-handed vulnerability to the inundation of God's love.

Such vulnerability is only possible in Jesus, the definitive expression of both the self-expending love of God and humanity's assent to that gift; Jesus not only models, but also mediates, being fully human. So becoming human involves a process of substitution: Jesus's surrendered heart replacing the ego and its ramparts. This transformation from self-sufficiency into Jesus's perfect "Yes" to God's love is the work of mystical grace. By

Rachel's account, then, the blossoming of the mystical life and human flourishing are one.

AN EMPTINESS TO RECEIVE PLENITUDE

Throughout these selections, Rachel emphasizes that humanity is an emptiness fundamentally oriented to receive the fullness of God's self-bestowing love.

If the heart of Christianity is the God who gives nothing less than God's own Self, it follows, as a logical conclusion, that the fundamental stance a Christian must take is that of receiving him. First and foremost we must accept to be loved, allow God to love us, let God be the doer, the giver, let God be God to us. But how hard it is for us to do that consistently! We are always reversing the role, intent on serving God, as we say, on doing things for God, offering God something. This is our natural bent, but it must be corrected by the vision of faith. Over and over again, Jesus tries to get his disciples to drop this self-import-ant attitude and to understand that, before God, they are only very small children who have no resources within themselves, but must look to their parents for everything, simply everything. It is not their role to give, but to receive. Jesus knows that this calls for a radical change of outlook and, more than outlook, a radical change of heart. From always trying to prove ourselves to God (is it not really to ourselves?), we have to become poor in spirit just as Jesus was. Jesus remained always a small child before his Father, always poor and dispossessed. The one thing in himself to which he draws attention is his meek and humble heart. How vividly John shows us the poverty of Jesus living only by the Father, disclaiming any life of his own, any personal resource. He is an emptiness into which the Father is always flowing, an unwritten melody waiting for him to sing.

—*EP*, 48–49

Man is the being to whom God cries, "Come to me." "Come, take possession of the kingdom prepared for you before the

foundation of the world." It was for this the world was made.
That there should be beings capable of receiving God, entering
into closest fellowship with him, sharing all God is and has. . . .

The call "Come to me" is not an afterthought as though God
first made man and then decided to call him to intimacy with
himself. This divine call is what constitutes man.   —*ICE*, 10

Jeremiah and all the Lord's prophets represent a band of faithful
ones who, baffled though they were by events and the seeming
absence of the Lord, struggled faithfully on in bitter suffering,
carrying forward for us the torch of divine revelation, men and
women "of whom the world was not worthy. . . . And all these,
though well attested by their faith, did not receive what was
promised, since God had seen something better for us, that apart
from us they should not be made perfect" (Heb. 11:38–40). With
our Christian insight, we discern a truth that is a continual challenge to each one of us. Israel was, indeed, God's chosen people
with a particular vocation, but it was for God, not for them, to
decide on how that vocation should be realized. They could not
see into the future and see how truly, how mysteriously, the great
promises to Israel would be fulfilled. The people of the past were
asked to accept God's mysterious ways in the night of faith:
"Trust me, leave yourselves in my hands." For very many, this
was too hard a saying. Faced with a crisis, against God's will,
they took the initiative, desperately trying to manipulate events
and even God himself, refusing to believe that he was their absolute savior and, if they would but trust him, ultimately, not a hair
of their head would perish. What matter if they were conquered?
What matter if they found themselves in the valley of darkness:
"I will be with you," and that is all that really matters to human
beings. Do we not see ourselves in these ancestors of ours?

Jesus' disciples were caught in a violent storm on the lake
and were sinking, while the Lord lay peacefully sleeping. Terrified, indignant, they shook him awake, reproaching him for his
indifference. There they were, desperately striving to keep from
sinking and he was doing nothing, sleeping! Jesus deflates their

high emotion with a reproach of his own. Why the panic? Where is your faith? Is he not saying: "Does it matter if you do go down provided I am with you?" How profound this is! "My ways are not your ways."

Are we not struggling ourselves, every day, to assimilate what the Lord was trying to teach his people long ago? Our only real need is God. We are made for God. Our destiny is in God and he created us in order to bring us to it. We persist in wanting to be god to ourselves, thinking that we know the shape of our destiny and how to reach it. Like our religious ancestors we are unable to believe that God will be God to us in every way if only we will let him.   —*LU*, 75–77

Our nature is to be all aspiration, a leaping upwards toward fulness of life in God; it is to be a purity able to reflect the beauty of God, an emptiness to receive plenitude.   —*AL*, 42

God is darkness in this life but a blessed darkness, a darkness our deepest self wants. Anything less than the all, which being no-thing, total mystery, must be darkness to us, would never satisfy us. We cannot have it both ways: a God made to our own measure, even our finest measure, whom we can grasp with our minds; and at the same time perfect human fulfillment. Loyally we must accept him in darkness, refuse to identify him with any means to him no matter how sublime and spiritual these may seem.   —*AL*, 73

Whatever we can grasp with our minds cannot be God. To grasp something means that we possess it, control it, that it is less than us. Such acquisitions can never satisfy the human spirit that is made for the infinite. Our longing, our need is for infinite Mystery and we can be satisfied with nothing less.

The *Creator almus siderum* [Creator of the stars of night] has become human. The cosmos itself is ultimately an impenetrable mystery. Science reveals facts that overwhelm our minds and imaginative faculties and can produce feelings of terror as well as wonder. Our existence, we ourselves are mystery and I do not see how we can be truly Christian without accepting and even rejoicing to live in mystery, knowing that all derives from and is encompassed by the one holy Mystery, whose human face it is given us to see and to recognize in it a limitless, selfless love.

—*LU*, 94

A SACRAMENT OF TRANSCENDENCE

The reverse side of being made to receive the gift of Godself is that nothing created will ultimately satisfy us. Our ego attempts to quell our gnawing sense of the insufficiency of all things with pretensions to self-fulfillment, however this sense is a sign, or sacrament, of our transcendence.

Revelation has shown us something we could not otherwise have known, that we are called not merely to a splendid human destiny of a kind we can appreciate and that, with God's help, we can gradually achieve, but to one that transcends any created nature whatsoever. We are called to share God's own life. We were created to receive uncreated life. Yet our nature, along with every creature that we know of on our planet, has an innate drive toward a fulfillment that is within its powers to attain. We humans are the only creatures who know they must die. Without faith's vision, human life is tragic. . . . All we have done to develop ourselves and the world around us eventually comes to nothing. We think of persons whom we have known and loved making a beautiful thing of their life, and must all this beauty, this mature love come to naught? Here lies the core of our human drama. *To come to our transcendent destiny we must renounce the powerful natural instinct to achieve a destiny by our own powers.*

We are open ended, a potentiality, a capacity for God, and when we allow ourselves to confront the reality of ourselves, we experience *emptiness, want, desire.* Ours is an incredibly wonderful vocation but a difficult one that involves an inescapable tension. One the one hand, we must accept our poverty, which is the sign or sacrament of our transcendence; acknowledging that, of ourselves, we can never attain our end. "Who then can be saved?" exclaimed the bewildered Peter. "It is impossible for man, but not for God for everything is possible to God" (Matt. 19:25–26; Mark 10:26–27; Luke 18:26–27). On the other hand, we are summoned to a great moral effort, conforming our lives to the demands of the gospel. Our natural powers must be developed to the full and we must devote ourselves to cooperating with God in the transformation of creation.   —*LU*, 147–48

The human heart . . . has a beloved, its first and only love, and he is the object of its desire. We are seeking him in all our seekings even when we betray him, substituting for him the myriad beauties of creation which he has set on our path to point us to him and kindle desire. We bear within our very substance an open wound of longing, dissatisfaction. We experience this but most often do not recognize its cause. . . .

    . . . [T]here is a fulfillment to our endless longing but not within ourselves, not within the limitations of this world or our own achievements, but as pure gift. There is an inevitable conflict between our true self and its deepest desire to be enfolded, possessed by our beloved, and the innate drive to control, possess, to find fulfillment within ourselves, of ourselves. This we can call the ego. It is our basic self-orientation which is a dead end. Let us say the true self is loyal to transcendence, the ego betrays and settles for limitation. . . . The self must triumph over the ego.

    . . . The ego curls inwards and, like a carnivorous flower, draws everything else within it, destroying both them and itself. This ego-centered movement is a perversion, it is disobedience in the fullest sense. It is sin. . . . Called beyond ourselves to the enfolding transforming love of the infinite, and never happy save in obedience to this call, we nevertheless shrink from commitment to it. Innately obstinate in us (and how strong!) is that which expects, demands, looks for fulfillment within this world, even though we know experientially and intellectually that it cannot be.

The New Testament speaks eloquently under different images of this perverse movement of the human spirit, this fundamental disobedience, this desire to be "god." It takes various forms, from crude materialism, "their gods are their bellies," to high spiritual pretensions; be it fervent keeping of the law and moral righteousness, or the denial of matter in favor of a "purely spiritual" religion of gnosticism. This is the "aeon" over which Satan rules (Eph. 2:2), the world which is the enemy of God. It is not the world of visible reality, God's beautiful creation which he finds "so good," but a realm of being that chooses to be subject to its own will alone. It chooses to settle within its own limited frontiers and thus be its own satisfaction, its own god. It is a denial of transcendence, a refusal to recognize fundamental, total dependence on God. Paul is only too aware of how all of us are caught in the meshes of this unholy web; it is an atmosphere we breathe from the moment we are born. It is a slavery though we know it not. "Who can deliver us?" cries Paul, and he answers with the triumphant cry of "Jesus." What can overcome the "world," the world that is the enemy of God? Faith—faith that acclaims Jesus as the Son of God.   —AL, 18–19, 21–22

It would be wrong to assume that what John [of the Cross] speaks of as dark night has nothing in common with ordinary non-religious human experience. The image is not alien. How many pages of literature, how many paintings and songs have as their theme a dark night when what once had meaning has none—when life's light has been extinguished, the heart bruised, the mind bewildered. Bereavement, disappointment, failure, old age, and, on the wider scene, the threat of atomic destruction, these and countless other common human experiences engulf us in night. All of them confront us with our finitude, raise fundamental questions on human existence and contain a challenge to accept our human vocation, whether we know the shape of that vocation or not. Every human being is for God and an openness for God. It is not only around us who know his name that the sun is shining but around every single person, seeking an entrance. He uses every occasion to illumine us and his illumination is most often perceived as darkness.   —*AL*, 57

BECOMING HUMAN

We are not born as fully realized human persons. We become human inasmuch as we resist being clothed in self-made grandeur and choose to stand naked before the outpoured love of God.

God's call to us to receive love and be drawn into sacred intimacy is what defines our humanness. But this relationship can remain undeveloped. A baby in its mother's womb is in relationship with her but is unaware of it and does not respond to the mother's intense love and desire to give herself to her child. The relationship with God on the human side can remain as minimal as that of the baby. Love must be freely given, freely received and freely returned.   —*LM*, 96

Our human lives here below consist of a succession of choices; we may never be static. We are "active" even in repose. John [of the Cross] gives a name to this human activity in so far as it is truly human, in so far as it is the appropriate response which brings a human being to its goal—faith. Faith is movement. It is the march of our feet toward our journey's end; it is the beat of our wings of transcendence, inseparable from hope and love. It is a going forth from our finite world into the infinite being of God. This fundamental choice is actualized in the thousand and one concrete details that fill our hours and days: duties faithfully carried out, acts of loving kindness, decisions for truth even in the smallest matters, self control . . . the list is endless. It is *living* faith that matters, not consciousness of faith, not a satisfying awareness of the security of faith. These may well accompany faith but they are not to be confused with it.   —*AL*, 104

What we have to do is see what Teresa [of Avila] is really saying
about the soul. She is saying that it is *for God*; it is a capacity
for God; he is its center and all its beauty is because of him. This
soul, this castle of immeasurable beauty and capacity is ourselves. It is there, this wonder, inviting exploration and possession even to the innermost room "where the most secret things
pass between God and the soul" and we are content to stay in the
outer courts if we choose to enter at all! For her, spiritual growth
is seen as a journey inwards, a penetration of this interior castle.
In her understanding, the castle is *already there*, our souls are,
so to speak, *ready made*, we have only to get to know them by
entering in. There is a problem but she avoids it by not seeing it!
But to say that we are not yet in our castle, at least not in any
but the outer-most court, is really saying the mansions are *not
there yet*, they come into existence. So important is this insight,
which Teresa grasped *practically* but did not express clearly in
her use of a static image, for understanding what she calls the
"supernatural work" of God and later calls infused or mystical
contemplation, to expound which, is her reason for writing the
book, that we must enlarge upon it.

Man, to use the classical expression, is a capacity for God.
Unlike every other form of life that we know of, he does not
come into the world ready made. The baby animal is animal,
whole and entire. It grows, reaches maturity and fulfillment
within the bounds of its own being and the world around it.
The human creature, this being made up of the same stuff as
the world and thrown up by its evolution, is not ready made. It
comes into the world incomplete, with no possibility of completion within itself or within the bounds of the material world. It
is a capacity, a possibility; a capacity that may never be filled, a
possibility that may never be realized, for, in this instance, the
creature has a choice. Man is a capacity for God, he comes into
existence insofar as he consents to be what he is, a "for-Godness." The human being is not a man until the possibility which
he is, is totally realized, the capacity which he is, is expanded to
its limits, "filled with all the fulness of God." Man, we maintain,

is not there yet. In Teresa's imagery, the mansions aren't there yet, just the foundation stones. They are to be built by the Master builder insofar as we consent to work with him. . . .

The idea that we are not there yet, that we have to become—shall we say, I have to become *me* and my *me* has to become God—finds firm basis in scripture in its talk of being born anew, a new creation, something wholly new and other coming into existence. The concept of the distinction between spirit and flesh is particularly important for our theme. For both Paul and John, "flesh" seems to indicate simply "what is not God." Thus the human being in itself is "flesh." "Spirit" stands for the God-realm. God is spirit, he alone can communicate spirit and what he touches becomes spirit. Never can "flesh" mount up to reach "spirit," "spirit" stoops down to touch "flesh," quickening it with new, "spiritual" life, which is the life of God himself. . . . Flesh and blood cannot penetrate the mysteries of God. All that can be said of man who is "flesh" is that he is open to spirit, he has the capacity to be touched by and transformed into spirit, becoming one spirit with the Lord who is Spirit. His whole destiny lies in being born again into spirit. . . . We are never allowing an opposition between soul and body. When we use spirit, or soul, (we choose to use them synonymously though Teresa makes a distinction between the two words) we mean the whole person insofar as they have been touched by God and are being transformed into spirit. It is only when flesh has become spirit totally that we have man. —*ICE*, 6–8

God is always working to bring us to an awareness and acceptance of our poverty, which is the essential condition of our being able to receive him, and the petty frustrations, the restrictions, humiliations, the occasions when we are made to feel poignantly and distressingly hedged around, not in control of the world, not even in control of that tiny corner of it we are supposed to call our own, are his chosen channel into the soul. It is the one who has learned to bow his head, to accept the yoke, who knows what freedom is. There is so much that we must take whether we like it or not; what I am urging is a wholehearted acceptance, a positive appreciation and choosing of this bitter ingredient of life.   —*TBJ*, 43

No one claims that of itself suffering purifies, but suffering patiently and bravely borne plays an indispensable role in human development. God offers himself to us at every moment, in our joys as well as in our sorrows, nevertheless there is a sense in which he offers himself more intimately in suffering. It is because in difficulty and suffering our hearts can be more open to receive him. We are painfully aware of our limitations and our need. Suffering creates a loneliness which others cannot penetrate; our sense of emptiness brings the realization that we can find no answer to the mystery of ourselves in this world. We are more likely to feel the need of a savior and open our hearts to him.

Long-drawn-out suffering that carries with it no element of self-satisfaction can be a special channel of God's entry into our hearts. Living for a long time with a difficult person, which demands a constant effort to be loving and understanding; temperamental difficulties which dog our footsteps, overshadowing us even on our brightest days; perseverance in a dull, demanding job, not merely for the sake of it but because duty demands. Then the still deeper suffering of seeing those we love in pain; lingering illness; anxiety about those we love; anxiety about our means of livelihood, fear of losing our job; bereavement which leaves an aching void for the rest of life. It is not the spectacular occasion which really costs, the sort of thing that suddenly lifts us out of routine and gives us the opportunity for splendid courage. It is amazing to what heroic heights ordinary people attain in time of crisis. But does this tell us much about the moral stamina of those involved? People who show up splendidly in crises can prove self-centered and childish in the ordinary rough and tumble of life. If we are looking for real heroism, the sort of heroism Jesus displayed, then we are likely to find it in some very ordinary man or woman, getting on with the job of living,

totally unaware that they are doing anything remarkable and
completely without pretension.   —*TBJ*, 74–75

Dearest Mark,

Who can explain precisely what we mean by "heart" and yet,
don't we all, instinctively, know? I avoid the very useful word
"soul" because it implies duality, that we are compounded of
body and that, whereas the body is mortal, the soul is immortal.
This leads us to the reassuring (?) conclusion that there is an
inalienable element in us that is of itself immortal. I cannot think
that this is true. The way I think about it is this. We are animals that can think and can choose. The fact that we can think
opens us to the infinite horizon of mystery. I believe that "from
the outset"—the scriptural "in the beginning" (meaning it never
was not so), human beings, these thinking animals are graced, in
relation to God . . . made for Yourself and ever desiring, restless,
seeking their absolute Love. The Light enlightens every mortal
being "from the outset." I think I would call that inmost desiring, yearning, the "heart." It is the effect of grace, of God's will
to draw us into his own life. It is rooted in the ability to choose,
in our freedom to choose.

Human beings desire happiness and are endlessly seeking for
it. They are longing for what is beautiful, good and, ultimately,
for what is absolutely so. In the measure that we choose rightly,
choose what is really true and good, we become ever more
authentically human and our Maker and Lover is able to communicate with us in increasing fullness. We become imbued with
eternal life, God's own life. Immortality is a pure gift. It does
not belong to our nature of itself. But our Creator and Lover
wants us and wants us "forever" with him; will never let us go,
be snuffed out, let us vanish like the grass of the field, because
he loves us. We have no other guarantee of life everlasting in
whatever form, except God's faithful love.

Is this a needless digression? Possibly. But it is led naturally
from my thinking of heart. Let's say "heart" is myself choosing;
let's say it is myself-in-God's-heart and always moved by God to

want him and to seek him. We can't take a peek inside and see
that self-in-God. And maybe this sense of unknowing, of obscurity regarding that inmost self, grows as we grow. . . .

With my love,
Ruth   —LP, 62–64

WE ARE IN CHRIST

*The process of becoming human explored in the previous pas-
sages occurs in Jesus, the one in whom humanity and divinity
are uniquely and perfectly united. Among the mysteries Rachel
contemplates here is that Jesus is found wherever there is genuine acceptance of our fragile humanity, even if there is no explicit
confession of him, and that the process of becoming human is a
process of deification.*

[O]nly in Jesus can we know the You who looks at me and says
the "you" that makes me the person I am. The great "You" and
the little "you" can be known only in Jesus.   —LP, 6

Jesus himself is the way; he is the mystery of God accessible to
us. He is also the archetype of human transcendence. John [of
the Cross]'s teaching is based on Jesus crucified. Everything in it
is to show us how to live as Jesus lived in total obedience to the
Father's call. In Jesus we learn what man is, what God intends
him to be. He never deflected from the "upward call," never
compromised with what would have detained him within the
limits of "the world." He never stood for himself, never claimed
self-sufficiency and independence. He saw himself always as an
emptiness for receiving his Father. Jesus "was made perfect,"
achieved the term of transcendence. In reaching the Father he
took us with him; and this marvelous work of reconciliation was
wrought, not when he was acting with power and performing
miracles, but when he was brought utterly low—emptied out,
annihilated.

Jesus is the way; he enables us to take the way he is. He is the door, the only door through which we reach the Father.

—*AL*, 7–8

We say we must feel fulfilled, that we have a right to this or that because we need it for our fulfillment. We must not be diminished or feel frustrated in our desires. But the truth is that we do not know what human fulfillment is. We can neither conceive of it nor the path to it except in Jesus and him crucified. To seek what we think is fulfillment, making it our sole aim and subordinating other people and things to our own needs is to lose our way. We must allow God to bring us to the fulfillment he has made us for, by a way that is infallible because it is his way for us. We must be brought to dispossession, emptiness, formlessness. A dreadful prospect? Does not this spell death to a human being? Paradoxically, no, it is the other side of the plenitude of life. It is to enter into him who is all, to be filled by the all.

—*AL*, 46–47

Just as no one can stand apart from the holy Mystery, neither can anyone not have to do with Jesus: every human person, just because a human person is a blood brother or sister of Jesus, is caught up into his life and destiny.   —*LM*, 33

[Jesus] accepted as none other ever can the essential poverty of the human condition and the working out of that in everyday life. He embraced it, but not without bitterness; he felt its sting as we do. To surrender to the embrace of the Father in which the human self joyfully, rapturously abdicates, is one thing; to surrender to him in the human situation as it is, besmirched, distorted by sin, is quite another matter, and Jesus felt the horror and injustice, the outrage of it.   —*TBJ*, 43

Jesus was utterly poor in spirit, the perfect Child of the Father accepting from the Father's hand his humanity in its limited, weak, and vulnerable condition. We have within us ingrained

ways of mitigating our poverty and for that reason cannot readily perceive that to be human is to be poor in the deepest sense. It
means depending for one's very existence on another in a world
that we do not control, exposed to the vicissitudes of nature, to
suffering of mind, emotion, and body. No one has accepted this
condition with such worshipful love as Jesus did. We reveal even
in early childhood an anger that things are not as I want them
to be and some of us carry throughout our lifetime a deep-down
resentment. Our ego insists on having its own way, manipulating
other people and circumstances to smooth its path and satisfy its
desires. Unless with Jesus, we lovingly accept the essential poverty of our humanity, acknowledging that our true security and
fullness of being are to be found only in the Father's under-gird-
ing arms, we can never really love. We will be irritable, quick to
take offense, resentful, unhappy.   —*QUD*, 42–43

It is by God's perfect will that each one of us exists: "I want *you*.
Be!" Existence is pure gift. "I" was not there to ask to be given
existence and life! Have you from time to time, or even once,
been confronted with the astounding *fact*: "I *am*, but I *need not
be*! I am *receiving* existence from my Creator! How close he is
to me!" Normally we take ourselves for granted but moments of
awed realization are precious.

Our life on earth begins as a tiny, helpless scrap of humanity,
totally dependant on others for the maintenance of life. From
the very first we are conditioned. We do not choose our par-
entage and all that involves in the way of race, homeland, and
culture. Our genes may be strong and healthy or they may be
defective. Our temperament is not of our choosing. Like all
mammals on earth given right conditions, our physical being
develops without any conscious intervention on our part. There
comes a moment however, when we humans can *choose* and it is
then that the great drama of our personal life begins, a drama of
such magnitude that only God can fully comprehend.

Created by Love and for Love, nothing on earth can ever fully
satisfy us. Still, we are creatures of earth, we love it, it is our

home, the maternal womb in which we are nourished and by which our needs are answered. Yet our deepest heart has a need that earth cannot fulfill, the need for God. We are of this world, adapted to it, drawn to it, yet called to a destiny that is beyond all created capacity to attain. This is our basic poverty. We *are* a yearning, an emptiness crying out to be filled by God. We long for something we have not got and, what is more, cannot get.

No such longings trouble the other inhabitants of our world. Their instincts direct them of necessity to their fulfillment within this world; born, they grow to maturity, reproduce, and die. Our grandeur and our pain is that, creatures of the earth that we are, our destiny is transcendent, beyond what we can know or, of ourselves, attain. Only God can bring us to God. We must allow him to and Jesus shows us the way the way of obedience.

Jesus' fundamental obedience that comprised all his distinct acts was to *accept* his humanity and experience without evasion the poverty and pain of being human. Each one of us is faced with the same choice: our Creator's loving will for us, or the vain pursuit of a fulfillment within this world? Although in prayerful moments, we sincerely determine to choose God's holy will, as our life unfolds day by day, we encounter the attraction of earthly things, the things seen rather than the things unseen known only by faith.

Constantly to choose in all the details of our life what faith shows us to be the will of God is impossible for us as of ourselves. The kenosis of Jesus alone enables us to do the impossible, to win the victory over our intense egotism, the self-centeredness that wants what *I* want here and now, the pride that claims independence. "Without me you can do nothing" (John 15:5).

Original sin is precisely a rejection of the true reality of our humanity that is to be a "*capax Dei*." As yet we are only in process of becoming human. We will be truly human when we are filled with the fullness of God. That can only be by denying our egotism and "letting" God, that is, by surrendering to his will. Jesus' life was one of total obedience to the Father's will even to a terrible, shameful death, to the loss of all that seemed to make him human—he was emptied. And that is why *the Father raised him to the heights* . . . filling his emptiness with himself. Obedience is faith and love in act.

In Jesus we see our path. He did not write his own script for the drama of his life and neither do we write ours. The part we must play is given to us. Our life's task is to devote ourselves to this, to be what God wants us to be, that unique, irreplaceable delight of his heart.   —*QUD*, 11–13

Jesus, in his Father's name, asks nothing save that we be truly human and he shows us how. . . . [B]ecause human fulfillment lies beyond the self and its egotism, which searches frantically within itself for its own immediate, comprehensible satisfaction, the acceptance of his teaching and of him, for he is his teaching, always demands humility, a bowing of one's neck to receive the yoke, an abdication of self in favor of him. This abdication is the essence of faith. It seems to me that wherever this acceptance of the human lot is found and in the measure that it is present, there is the Lord. An explicit acknowledgement of him is not necessary. In embracing what is truly human Jesus is embraced.

I suspect that this is often the case and there can well be more true acceptance of him in people who do not explicitly acknowledge him than in many who do, yet continually evade life and "what is," often in his name. These others obey an inner urge which assures them there is meaning somewhere and that what they must do, the demand of their humanity, is to refuse to slump down in self but to surrender to life, bravely confronting it as it is and bowing before that which they cannot overcome.
                                                        —*TBJ*, 44–45

As Jesus shared our flesh and blood in the time of his kenosis, now that he is glorified we share his divine life, a life that belongs to no creature by nature, but is proper to God alone. This life comes to us through Christ.

To say Christ is our representative and all he did was as our representative is inadequate. More is involved. In a way we cannot fully grasp, we are "in" Christ, incorporated in him. God has given him to us as our High Priest, as our Head and, in solidarity with him, "through him, with him and in him" we are able to offer God perfect atonement, perfect worship, a love that is worthy of him. So it is that through God's wonderful devising, it was man, one of us, who by his unparalleled, humble, unswerving obedience brought us home to our God and our Father. . . .

"(God) is the source of your life in Christ Jesus, whom God made our wisdom, our righteousness and sanctification and redemption" (1 Cor. 1:30). All is *gift*. Nothing is wanting to us. We have been given the right to a marvelous inheritance, nothing less that the inheritance of Christ: "all that is mine is yours" (Luke 15:31); "the glory which thou has given to me I have given to them" (John 17:22); "heirs of God and joint heirs with Christ" (Rom. 8:17), can we even begin to penetrate the implications of this? People of deep prayer and some theologians have used the bold term "deification" as the only adequate way of expressing this work of God. The human self has to "die" in the sense that it must surrender completely to the divine embrace. This divine embrace purifies and transforms it. God works, and God's work is God.

Only when we have died with Christ, been buried with him, and risen with him, will we be truly human. Now we are in the process of becoming.   —*LU*, 136–37

We cannot be true to our humanity made in the image of God unless we live a life like God's life of self-expropriation in bestowal to others. We can become our true selves only by giving our selves away, living for God and for others. To cling to self, to remain in self can end only in death, in a hell of our own choosing. True life, eternal life is life in communion, for the Fount of all existence is Communion: "that they may all be one; even as thou Father, art in me, and I in thee" (John 17:21). "In the image of God he made them"!

How deeply St. Paul entered into this mystery! To him was revealed the unsearchable riches of Christ and the human

vocation to be "in Christ." He saw and lived the practical consequences of this. Jesus had promised his apostles a share in the
chalice of his suffering (cf. Matt. 20:23) and in the Letters of St.
Paul we get a glimpse of the share that was his, see for instance,
2 Cor. 1:8–11; 11:16–33; 12:5–10. The encounter with the risen
Lord shattered the self-assured, self-righteous Saul; stricken
with an incurable wound, like Jacob before him he went his
way limping, no longer Saul but Paul (Gen. 32:24–28). Face to
face with Jesus, his spiritual destitution was revealed to him. He
confronted his sinfulness and total inability to save himself. The
image of God he had inherited or fashioned for himself, was
shattered:

> I had heard of thee by hearing of the ear,
> but now my eye doth see thee;
> therefore I despise myself
> and repent in dust and ashes. (Job 42:5, 6)

Rather than sinking into despair he learned to "boast" of his
weakness, knowing that Christ's power would be free to work
and that magnificently, through his very weakness. "When I am
weak then I am strong" (2 Cor. 12:10). This does not mean he
experienced *himself* as strong, most likely he continued to feel
weak and fearful but he was certain that the *divine* weakness
and powerlessness of love by which we were redeemed, was
invincible. St. Thérèse of Lisieux had a profound understanding
of this paradox. The poorer we are without inner resources, the
more Jesus can work in us. She is emphatic that the greatest of
all the graces God gave her was to show her her weakness and
to inspire her with an unshakeable trust in his infinite mercy. The
more wretched we are the more God is free to give himself to
us provided we accept our poverty and throw ourselves in total
trust into the arms of his merciful love. "O my divine sun, I am
happy to feel myself so small and frail in your presence and my
heart is at peace" (St. Thérèse of Lisieux).

Silent, hidden, powerless Love, the world does not recognize
you but by your gift we recognize you and fall in silent worship.

We entreat you to draw us, wrest us away from our self-centered selves and assume us into yourself. May we seek ourselves in nothing, but by living by you and in you, devote ourselves entirely to the fulfillment of your holy will. O humble, powerless Love, yours is the kingdom, the power, and the glory forever and ever! —*QUD*, 51–52

If we want God to be our All then our ego has to die. If we are to live by divine energy, then we must surrender—allow divine Love to take away (or, rather, transform) our own inner springs. It means we must stop clinging to our own perceptions, demanding to stay within our own capabilities, insisting on a deity we can manage. We have to accept to have nothing whatsoever of our own. Since our profoundest reality, our for-Godness, is concealed from normal perception and is a pure gift of God that we cannot manipulate or "possess," so the mysterious work of our transformation and the substitution of the divine for the merely human, take place in deepest secrecy. Blind trust in Love can be the only answer. —*LM*, 101

[I]n spite of accurate theological knowledge of [Jesus'] absolute and unique mediatorship, in practice, many of us have the secret notion that we are working to get beyond this to a "pure" prayer where "God" is experienced directly, where we no longer need Jesus. We are failing to see the import of Jesus' words that to see him is to see the Father, that to know him is to know the Father, that to be in him is to be in the Father and that we have no direct link with the Father, if by "direct" we mean other than through Jesus. We want to think we have but we have not. "No one can come to the Father but by me," and this, not in the sense that you use me to get to him and when you have got to him you don't need me anymore, but you have simply no contact with the Father except through me in time and in eternity. But of course, this *is* direct contact. Jesus' communication *is* "pure God" and only his communication is "pure God." What we call the mystical, a direct, unmediated contact with God, *is* Jesus. He is his living touch. We have this direct contact only in him. . . . [H]is life is secretly, escaping our consciousness, substituting itself for ours. We are becoming Jesus. . . .

. . . Jesus *is* surrender, and what he shows us, what he enables us to do, is to surrender also. We have no other objective in this life; it is the fulfillment of our nature to effect this surrender. We are only human when we have completely forsaken ourselves in love. The other side of fulfillment—the Father's answer—is not our business. Our whole intent as Jesus' was must be to surrender no matter what the cost. We are absolutely certain as he was of ultimate fulfillment because of his Father's love. He trusted his Father, he did not seek to peer into the future to see the form of this fulfillment; he was too absorbed, too in love to look beyond his present task of surrender. . . . Jesus is effecting his own surrender in us, drawing us away from all self-interest, making his love ours. It is a profound sharing in his death, but a death that is only the reverse of life.   —*ICE*, 107–9

For mystical life, infused contemplation, these things mean absolutely nothing to me unless they mean Jesus and his life in us; Jesus who alone brings God and man together; Jesus our holiness. . . .

. . . The mystical life is beyond our power, nothing we can do can bring us to it, but God is longing to give it to us, to all of us, not to a select few. He made us for this, to share his divinity, to become his sons and daughters in very truth, with all that this implies. The prerequisite on our part is an acceptance of poverty, of need, of helplessness; the deep awareness that we need Jesus our savior who alone brings God and man together, who is our holiness. . . .

We are eager to stress that the mystical is of the essence of Christianity, not the privileged way of the few. To be more precise: it means being wholly possessed by God and that is holiness. One cannot be holy unless one is a mystic and if we do not become mystics in this life we become such hereafter.

—*GMP*, 1, 6, 10

DISTINCT STAGES OF NEARNESS TO GOD

In these selections, Rachel uses various images to establish that the process of becoming human, the process of being taken into Jesus's definitive surrender to the Father's inundation of love, is a three-stage journey.

[T]he division of our spiritual journey into three stages is no fanciful fabrication but arises from the very nature of things, God being what he is and we being what we are. They are distinct stages of nearness to God. To begin with we have not yet "come" to Jesus even though we are in his company and want to learn from him. Like Nicodemus we draw near to Jesus in our night of ignorance. Not that Nicodemus thought himself ignorant! We make an act of faith, an all-important, primal one, "We know that you are a teacher come from God." Jesus, in mysterious language, tries to make Nicodemus understand what must happen if he is to go further, if he is to enter the kingdom, that sphere where God, not man, is in supreme control, where God gives and man receives. The master of Israel must, like Paul, lay aside his own ideas and consent to become a little child. Nicodemus considers himself a virtuous, wise man and Jesus is telling him this wisdom and virtue will get him nowhere. He is still trapped in the sphere of the flesh, and flesh can never attain God. In the word "flesh" there is no suggestion of body as distinct from spirit. What is meant is man as he is in himself, left to his own resources, or rather choosing to depend on his own resources, for God is always offering to take over. Jesus impresses on this great man his complete helplessness in the things of God. You cannot control the wind nor predict its movements, neither are you in control of the Spirit; you have to surrender to his control. Nicodemus has to die to his own life and be born again, otherwise he can never enter the kingdom.

For one who accepts this way of surrender, there follows a long and arduous discipleship. Perfect transformation into Jesus does not take place all at once. Man must co-operate with the action of the Holy Spirit who is now able to operate freely from within, where before he could only direct the mind and heart from outside. Now the heart has opened to receive him. This is the second stage, true discipleship. This long discipleship will most surely lead to the last stage, transforming union, which is what Christianity is all about.   —*TBJ*, 30–31

At the beginning of our spiritual journey John [of the Cross] bids us take Jesus as our model, bids us have an avid appetite to imitate him in everything, constantly meditate on him. When we have grown spiritually we are invited to a deeper intimacy, a deeper sharing. John points us to Jesus in the great act of redemption, stripped of all, emptied out, brought to nothing. If we are to receive all God wants to give us we too must enter into this mystery of self-emptying.   —*AL*, 96

It is as if God endows us with wing structure. We have to work the muscles of these embryonic wings to make them develop but no matter how much we try, we cannot get off the ground, that is, away from self. When the wings, through exercise, are sufficiently grown, then comes a divine influence, a wind that not only uplifts us but something of its strength penetrates the wings themselves so we can begin to fly, leaving self behind first from time to time, then for longer periods. Thus eventually we are in the painful condition of not being wholly in self and yet not belonging wholly to God. We are still within the influence of the earth, pulled back by gravity even though we are moving toward God. If we are faithful there will come a moment when God will stoop down, catch hold of us and sweep us up to himself, taking us right away from earth (self), so definitively that its power over us is lost for ever; there is no return. Henceforth we live with and in God. His powers, not our own, control all our activities. No effort of ours can achieve it. It is he himself who must snatch us away from ourselves.   —*TBJ*, 91

4

Opening to the Gift of God

To begin with we have not yet "come" to Jesus even
though we are in his company and want to learn from
him.   —*TBJ, 30*

In this chapter and the next, we experience Rachel as something
of a formator in the ways of the spiritual life. We are guided
here, not unlike her novices, through the fragile beginnings of
our openness to God's self-bestowal; this is the first stage of our
transformation into Jesus. If mysticism is being taken directly
into the life of Jesus and, in him, receiving the gift of God's outpoured love, then this is the "pre-mystical" stage of the spiritual
journey.

Rachel details that we are initially on the outskirts of the
self-emptying Jesus, so to speak. While there is some unfurling
of our innate orientation to self-satisfaction, the ego is still in
the ascendancy. Created to be filled with the fullness of God, to
remain at this stage is to betray our deepest human identity.

The great value of this chapter is the comprehensive and practical advice Rachel gives concerning anticipating the dawning
of God's gratuitous mystical grace. She urges a wholehearted
generosity, a going to the utmost of our limits, in coming to
know and imitate Jesus's self-abandoning surrender to God's
love. While we can never elicit the direct divine intervention that
transforms the ego into receptivity, these efforts are the necessary preparation for this grace.

Transformation necessarily calls for pu
burned away; there must be a dying to
in order to live with the life of Jesus. It is
close that so many of us turn back, or at leas
a little parable will illustrate the paradox. We
of making a lamp for God to shine in. We set t
in devotional exercises, in serving our neighbor,
selves, and, in a word, doing all the good that lie
Then we ask: "What is yet wanting?" The answer
carry your lantern up the mountain to offer it to m

So, carrying our precious, beautifully crafted lante
cost so much labor, we set out. As we progress, my
our lamp loses its luster. Why, it is tawdry! So tawdry
that we are tempted to turn back to make another or e
the one in our hands. Many do yield to this impulse an
spend their lives making their lantern beautiful so as to be
thy of God. Others, possibly only a few, go on, painfully a
of the pathetic nature of what they are offering, but they th
to themselves: God can shine in anything; his shining will
the more evident in this poor, misshapen tin than in a bejewele
lamp of gold. So, trustingly, on they trudge, thinking more of
God than of their gift. It may then come to pass that a dark
cloud overshadows them and a voice from the cloud says: "Now,
drop your lantern."

Narrow is the gate, strait the way that leads to life, it allows
for no baggage, no spiritual acquisitions and no swollen self-importance. It is for the "little ones." . . .

We have a choice: *to believe* the God who has shown himself
to us, deny self and its subjectivity, which, of course dominates
our consciousness, drop our "lantern," surrender and plunge
into the holy mist, or we can go on clinging to self, fashioning
a holiness of our own which, with its illusion, its fears and burdens, cannot glorify the Father. The choice is ours.

—*LU*, 151–52, 158

AWAKENING TO FAITH

*This section surveys a variety of topics. The unifying theme
is the mystery of awakening to faith. Rachel considers coming to belief from nonbelief, and the shift from being "religious" to being a disciple of Jesus. We also see that, while
ego bound, the various people at the first stage of the spiritual journey know some nascent movement away from total
self-preoccupation.*

What Is Faith? What Does It Mean to Have It or to Lack It?

Faith is a profound mystery that we can never adequately
explain. It is an interplay between divine grace and the human
mind and will. We are speaking of Christian faith, and that is
faith in Jesus Christ as the incarnate Word of God. The object of
our Christian faith is the God revealed in Jesus Christ.

Faith is never a mere intellectual assent but always involves
commitment. It is always in action, more a verb than a noun.
Faith cannot be one facet or a particular aspect of my life,
but my whole life. As St. Paul says, "My real life is the faith I
have in the Son of God who loved me and delivered himself
for me."

It is the Holy Spirit who enables us to believe—"No one can
come to me except the Father that sent me draw him"—but we
must cooperate with all our powers. And this means we must
"labor for the food which endures to eternal life" (John 6:27).
"This is the labor of God that you believe in him whom he has
sent" (John 6:29). What can be more important?

Many people think they have no faith because they feel they
haven't. They do not realize that they must make a choice to
believe, take the risk of believing, of committing themselves and
setting themselves to live out the commitment. Never mind that
they continue to feel that they do not believe. Under cover of
being "authentic" we can spend our lives waiting for the kind of
certainty we cannot have.

What, Then, Is Doubt?

I do not see how we can talk of faith if we eliminate the possibility of doubt. We cannot have the certainties that our nature craves and finds in the evidence of the senses. Perhaps most of the time we do not advert to doubt, but at times it can press heavily. As far as I am concerned, troublesome feelings of doubt seem a matter of the imagination failing to cope. Although we have no scientific verification for what we believe, there is nothing irrational in Christian faith but an enormous amount of data to support it.

In times of difficulty my anchorage is the Gospels. There I encounter Christ, "Light most beautiful," who overcomes the darkness of doubt. My faith is essentially faith in Jesus Christ: "You are Truth. Your word is truth and what is troubling me is a lie." I believe that there comes a point when a person is so held by God that, no matter how assaulted that person may be, faith stands firm, for "no one can snatch them from the hand of my Father" (John 10:29).   —GW, 10–11

Recently I was saddened on reading a letter from a young man I have known since he was a schoolboy and is now a husband, and father of three infants. He writes: "I am frightened. Much of what I believed in my life is crumbling. A religion I once held dear no longer makes sense to me." The word "religion" is significant. There is a vast difference between religion and faith in the God revealed in Jesus Christ, or, as a dear friend of mine expresses it, there is a vast difference between being religious and being a true disciple of Jesus. In the first instance, being a faithful Christian seems to consist in living a good moral life, practising justice and love toward others, and faithfully observing certain religions practices. Praise indeed, for those who live so! They are precious to God and he longs to give them so much more. The inner disturbance and distress this young man is feeling could well be the secret call of the Spirit to go beyond the externals to a purer, deeper faith, to an encounter, mysterious by its very nature, with the living and true God revealed in Jesus Christ.

Often and often I have reflected on what can be done to ensure the seismic shift from being just religious to ardent discipleship. Does it rest entirely on zealous teaching, preaching or even example? It seems not. Those of us, who by God's mercy may claim that they really desire to be disciples, can no doubt recall the "moment" when in some way they saw, or more truly they were shown, they were awakened. The "moment" may have been an extended moment or a stunning lightning flash. Dramatic or not, the heart of it was: I was blind and now I see. God really matters! We know that we must change, that much in our conduct and attitudes is not good.

Responding thus to this new vision, which is nothing less than an encounter with the Lord, is what he means by, "Do penance, for the kingdom of God is at hand." How profound, how precious a grace! It is indeed the pearl of great price. Why is it given to some and not to others? We do not know. Listening to the stories of aspirants to our monastery I have discerned no pattern. This one comes from an explicitly atheistic family, educated to be a very moral atheist, while that one comes from nominal Christianity and religious indifference. Rare today is one whose childhood faith and practice have matured along with her natural growth, and then found her vocation as a Carmelite. When I have been told these stories of conversion and read of others, I know that I am confronted with miracles of grace for which one can only give thanks.

Why is it that, in a devout family, some of the children remain steadfast in faith and others do not? Why does one young person show signs of more than ordinary spiritual insight and spiritual desire? We simply do not know. Is the offer made to all in varying degrees and in various guises, but ignored by some or even knowingly and willfully rejected? Again, we do not know. Jesus gives us the parable of the seed lavishly sown, which clearly indicates the part played by human responsibility in the seed's fruitfulness. However, there are many texts to infer invincible human ignorance and therefore lack of responsibility in individuals. It is the disciples' task to do something about this: "[H]ow are they to believe in him of whom they have not heard (have never been shown what he is like)? And how are they to hear without a preacher?" (Rom. 10:14). Again, "Let your light so shine before men, that they may see your good works and give glory to your Father, who is in heaven" (Matt. 5:16). What is more, Jesus makes it clear in his picture of the judgment (Matt. 25), that many know, love and serve him without knowing his name. The human heart is God's most secret domain. We may never judge another because we simply cannot.

What we must be certain of is that the pure, totally unmerited grace we have received, if it is indeed the pearl of great price to be guarded with our very life, is a talent that must be put to use. It is not given for ourselves alone but for others. To be a Christian is to be a missionary. . . . Maybe someone is thinking sadly: "I have received no call. I wish I had." Be certain that to think it, to want it, is the call. His loving gaze rests on you. You have no excuse. Gird your loins and follow the Lord!   —*LU, xv–xix*

What a vast land is this first island and how densely populated! It can be presumed that the great majority of men and women dwell on it. Its inhabitants range from those with the crudest of moralities, following their feebly-lit, maybe erroneous conscience, to those who like the young man in the gospel, can sincerely say of the commandments of God, "all these have I kept from my youth." But God doesn't want us to stay here; he didn't create, didn't redeem us for this. . . . We *can* move off it. Oh, not of our own ability, only God can enable us to transcend its bounds, but he is all eagerness to do so. . . .

Of course, we must allow for the possibility of sinners, believers or unbelievers, for those who have deliberately chosen to dwell in the caverns underground, but how easily we can be mistaken in pointing to them. The more I have looked at the world of men, read history, novels, case-histories of crime, the more convinced I am that man is not wicked but blind. Often you get the impression that mankind is wandering blindly and aimlessly in a great, dark forest, getting entangled, falling into pits, with no sense of direction; not wicked but blind and helpless. God has given some of us lanterns to bear in this dark forest, lighting up the path for others. We are endowed with the mental and psychic health denied to many, a good background, education, let alone spiritual insight, and it is we who are more likely to be sinners.

As I said, if I confine my references and instances to religious life, it is simply because this is the situation of which I have living knowledge, not because what I am writing about concerns religious only. Far from it; others can make their own application. My worry when I allow my mind to consider sinners would be the slack religious, the one who has been given a lamp which she has allowed to go out. There may be nothing outrageous, just a persistent choosing of self in small ways, shown by a grumbling, discontent, the attitude which judges everything by whether I *like* it: horarium, office, community functions, human contacts, food; if any do not please, if they disturb or inconvenience, then there are complaints, either externally or within, according to temperament. There is a bitterness which is an infallible indication of selfishness. One must question whether such a one is in a state of grace. Can one continually choose self even though the occasions be small and still be in a state of friendship with God? Isn't this to choose dwelling in the underground caverns?

—*GMP*, 15–16

Can we conceive of a human being who has not one spark of goodness in him, who is mere smoking flax . . . but this, we are told, is precisely what Jesus will nurture and not put out. It might be no more than kindness to a bird or animal but in so far as it is goodness, in so far as it is human, it is truly godly, truly "heaven" and heaven belongs to heaven. —*TBJ*, 108–9

GOD HAS A RIVAL IN THE EGO

Through the next set of passages, Rachel paints for us a spiritual portrait of those at the beginning of the spiritual journey. We see that, basically self-possessed, God can only relate to them indirectly, through created realities. Furthermore, this stage emerges as one of paradoxical spiritual self-confidence. Given that beginners live wholly from the ego, rather than with the life of Jesus, they live with a God made in their own image whose system of transactions is within their scope of control.

They still approach God in Old Testament fashion by ignoring Jesus. Such persons would be shocked to have it put thus but it is the truth. They seek for clear knowledge apart from him, they seek it in signs and tokens and interior assurances. They want to uncover mysteries. They disdain ordinary reason and the natural law expecting to receive knowledge and guidance direct from God. . . .

Instead of darkness and not-knowing these people want clear knowledge; instead of poverty and humiliation they want to possess secrets; instead of struggle and affliction they want consolations; instead of the hard labor of acquiring virtue they want sweetness in prayer. They are bypassing Jesus, settling within the confines of created things, managing themselves, basically seeking themselves. This is not to enter into the mystery of the crucified Jesus.   —AL, 96–97

What we call the history of salvation is enacted, or should be, in every human heart. There is the stage of preparation, of promise. God sets to work to educate his sinful people, to give them some sort of knowledge of what he is like so that they can imitate him. It would be impossible without this long preparation for man to recognize, still less accept God as he is in himself. He reveals himself in signs and figures; through the events of history he trains and forms his people until the time has come for his direct intervention. . . .

. . . Just as the vast numbers living in the era of Jesus histori-
cally speaking were not so in reality but still in the era of the Old
Testament, so with us. Each of us begins in the Old Testament
and maybe we never move out of it in this life; it will depend on
our desire. We are invited to do so—the preparation is preparation *for* something, not a value in itself. To move out of it
involves really accepting Jesus and this means "earthquake," the
overturning of our world, the end of it, a death in order to rise to
the new life in Jesus, which means that then we will be *in reality*
in the era of Spirit. —*ICE*, 54–55

[T]here is no spiritual "depth" for God to touch directly; he can
only communicate with the reality that is there, and this is material. Teresa [of Avila] points out that God's appeals come through
the body, through the senses, by means of good conversations,
sermons, books, good thoughts and feelings, sickness, trials, and
other events of life. She is careful to note that there is a different
mode of divine communication but this is for later on. Thus,
[this stage] is distinguished from later ones by the fact that God
can communicate himself only *indirectly*; but, and this is what
matters, he is bent on bringing us on, he wants our growth, he
wants the seed to germinate beneath the soil, to put down its tap
root, to feed on the salts, until it is ready for its contact with the
sun, then it can burst through the dark earth at the call of the
sun to receive its life-giving rays. This stage cannot be skipped.
It is not a question of God withholding his graces from some
and giving them to others so that some are bathed in sunshine
from the start. God is always giving himself but we must grow
to receive him. Were the germinating seed exposed too soon to
the rays of the sun it would be destroyed. —*ICE*, 21–22

To live by "flesh" is to live within the limits of our own potential, within the limits of our own perception and understanding,
according to how things seem and feel, according to our natural
experience. It is instinctive for us to live thus, taking for granted
that our conscious experience is to be trusted, that it is the way

things really are, the way we are, the way God is—that this *is* our life. We want to remain on this level because it is within our grasp; it is "ours" and affords a sort of security and assurance. This is so natural to us, even to us religious people, that we are unaware of how much of our life is lived from self, relying on self and not on faith in the Son of Man. We cannot rid ourselves of this deeply rooted pride and self-possession by our own strength. Only the Holy Spirit of the Crucified and Risen One can effect it, and this he is indeed always trying to do. But we must recognize his work, and respond "Amen."   —*EP*, 78

We long to work as equal partners with God and we do not want something for nothing because then we would have no guarantee that we would get it. We can rely on our own reliability but not on God's! We like to feel sure that, if we have done our duty well, kept the law, lived to the best of our lights, everything must be alright. Justice is satisfied; not even God can ask more. God owes it to us to see that we get a just reward!

Divine Love knocks at our defended heart; the Strong One attempts to break in but we can be so set about with our securities that he withdraws defeated. Like Jesus' contemporaries, we do not want to feel the ground shift beneath our feet. We do not want to admit that we need a new orientation. Behind all this is our dread of uncertainty, our dread of mystery. We want to be told exactly what is right and what is wrong, what we must do and what we must avoid. We want authoritative assurances. If we do not find them within ourselves we hope to get them from someone else. But no one can give us the certainties we crave. We already have the only certainty there is and the only one we need, an absolute Guarantor of love and fidelity and it is by this Holy One we must live in peace and security.

Our fears, our yearnings for assurance, reveal clearly that we do not believe in God's unconditional love. If we really do believe then we can live happily without certainties, with no anxieties about failures.   —*LM*, 78–79

Though the third mansion is a state that ought not to be, Teresa [of Avila] has to admit that it seems the normal state of most good people and so she gives it her attention, diagnosing its weakness.

She begins by praising those who have reached this stage: the bewildering and deceptive thing about it, is that there seems much to praise. If we meet people who have overcome their bad habits, who live carefully ordered lives materially and spiritually, whom nothing would induce to sin, who love doing penance, spend hours in recollection, who use their time well, practice works of charity toward their neighbor and are very careful in their speech and dress, would we think them not only admirable but saintly? Aren't we inclined to say "so and so is a perfect saint"? Teresa doesn't think so and her exposé of this state is one of her most fruitful contributions to the understanding of what growth in the spirit really is. It is because this state seems so good and exemplary, that it is a stumbling block to true holiness. Too often this third mansion in real life is taken to be the summit of the spiritual life: it tends to satisfy us and those around us yet it is far from what Christianity is all about. Teresa is happier and more at ease writing of the second mansion. It is truer, healthier. There we are consciously struggling with sin that humiliates us. In the first mansion, because there is no light, we can overestimate ourselves, but in the second we have become exposed to the light a little and this inevitably is humiliating. If this first gleam of self-knowledge and humility are absent then we are not in the second mansion.

Teresa has already warned us of the need for welcoming, never shirking, the painful awareness of our sinful self. But alas, this is a hard thing for us humans because we don't know God, we don't really believe in his unconditional love no matter how much we say that we do. To stand before him as we are in our naked shame, and not to run away and hide, or deck ourselves in our fine thinking to conceal our poor reality, we have to believe in his love. We reduce God to our own likeness, and this in great measure, I think, because we have not taken the trouble to go to the source, to find out for ourselves in the scriptures, and above all in Jesus, what he is really like. We prefer to live with our preconceived notions or with what others communicate to us, and the result is a caricature of God which at one and the same time gives us comfort because, having him in our image, we can cope with him; and despair because, again seeing him in our own image, we feel he hates us for our ugliness. Therefore we can't afford to be ugly, we have to hide it from ourselves and so we bury it all deep down; we bury the gnawing doubts and fears, and manage to achieve a state of relative self-satisfaction. Our seemingly excellent behavior gives support to this self-satisfaction. It is of enormous consequence to us that we behave well, that our thoughts, desires, actions are those of a "spiritual person." Tremendous inner energies are at work to produce this "perfection" which has in fact nothing to do with true growth.

What has happened is that the roots of our basic selfishness have been left untouched. This selfishness takes ever more subtle forms which, because they are subtle, do not cause the humiliation and shame of grosser manifestations. This is the danger Teresa is alive to. . . .

Virtue is often more apparent than real, the roots of sin remain strong and tenacious but the foliage, for the present, looks alright. We are deceived because we want to be, being more concerned with our own spiritual image than in becoming all God's. We have a deep secret satisfaction with ourselves; we do really feel we are advanced though would never say so even to ourselves. We practice the externals of humility and this means humble acknowledgements about self, our faults, our lack of progress; Oh yes, we are poor sinners! But we don't really think so. Teresa helps us to recognize our illusion and if we study the examples she gives with great care, we can learn a lot.

Here is someone who automatically puts everything in an edifying context. A spade is never a spade. He doesn't want to recognize his covetousness and lack of detachment, and his self-esteem finds ways of explaining to himself why he feels and acts as he does. No one can offer advice because he knows all there is to know, after all, he is an adept at the spiritual life, he can give good advice to others. The aches, pains, humiliations which flow from the simple realities of human life or from his own self-esteem become "suffering for God." Everything, everything becomes perverted and made a sop for self-esteem. He just can't take the lessons Our Lord is trying to teach. Teresa turns on her own daughters lest they should be complacently thinking this example has nothing to do with them after all, they don't have property to lose, they have no worldly ambitions. She points out how the same vices are in them. Watch those seemingly trifling incidents, a slight that arouses my indignation, note how I stand on my dignity, claim my little rights, how I think I have a *right* to feel wronged because I have been passed over, removed from a particular job, left aside, not appreciated as I think I ought to be. If we were to make a fuss in public then we would feel shamed because our weakness would be revealed, but when the wrong reactions are concealed by pieties, grace of manner, subtleties, then we feel no shame whatever. We don't think they matter. Teresa is quite obsessed, we shall find, by this basic concern for our "honor." She sees it as *the* problem—an underlying lack of humility. She worries because it is so common as to be accepted as normal and it is not seen as the vice it is. It is merely "human," smiled at in others, compatible with holiness because we accept it in ourselves. Few realize its importance. The whole law of growth is movement away from self. If the growing point of a seed were to remain folded up within the acorn it would come to nothing. It has to uncurl, push itself out, up and away. We can only become by leaving ourselves. Here we are choosing to stay in self. We have tidied self up, made it respectable and possible to live with and now we settle down, not prepared for that total forsaking of self, that total love of neighbor which is true growth in the spirit. We are clinging to the world of "flesh and blood" as Paul would say, deciding to stay in the womb. Deciding? Yes, a

choice is being made. It is we who are choosing to shut out the
call, the creative call to a wholly new life, a new way of being,
the way of "spirit."   —ICE, 28–31

All three writers of the Synoptic Gospels reveal Jesus' insistence
on the necessity of becoming as little as a little child in order to
enter the kingdom of God. This is a sharp-edged utterance and,
when understood, is likely to provoke as strong a reaction as
when Jesus insisted: "Unless you eat the flesh of the Son of man
and drink his blood, you have no life in you."

"This is a hard saying," many exclaimed; "Who can listen
to it?"(John 6:60). And they deserted Jesus. We are wise to
reflect and consider if we too, confronted with the full reality
of becoming as a little child, are severely tempted to "walk no
more with him."

Jesus' disciples left the security of family, home and livelihood to throw in their lot with Jesus. In regard to this world,
they are poor and powerless, little ones of no account, and
Jesus is grateful for their loyalty and courage. However, he
has no illusions: their self-interest has merely shifted from this
world to the mysterious kingdom that their master is inaugu-
rating. What gleaming crown awaits them?

To reach a deep understanding of this "hard saying," we
have to ask what Jesus means by the kingdom of heaven. He
is not talking only about the heaven awaiting us when we die;
he is talking about the now. In his own historical context, he
understands that the work his Father has given him to do is to
draw Israel back to God, to renew it and shape it to become all
that God intended it to be for the salvation of the nations. In
his person the reign of God begins.

"Our God reigns! Our God reigns," we sing lustily enough,
but does he? Does God reign fully in his Christian people?
Does God reign in our hearts, every day, every hour of the
day in every circumstance? To acknowledge God as king, to
enthrone God in our hearts means accepting to be spiritually
helpless, to be little, unimportant, totally dependent. It is to

dethrone the ego. To become as a little child has everything to do with the first and greatest commandment: "You shall love the Lord your God, with your whole heart, with your whole soul and with your whole strength . . . and you shall love your neighbor as yourself."

"I believe in one God," we say in the Nicene Creed. But in every human heart without exception, God has a rival in the ego. No one can serve two gods at one time. Jesus tells us that it is impossible to see the kingdom, let alone receive or enter it, without a radical renunciation of our natural self-possession and instinctive self-glorification. Given the world as it is, given the way we are, God's kingdom cannot come without renunciation and suffering.

Only our Creator knows who and what we are and the glory and blessedness God destines for us. On our own we cannot know any of this and certainly cannot achieve our proper fulfillment. It can come about only by self-surrender in total trust to our Creator, doing God's will, which has no other object than our blessedness. As I understand, there are two major effects of the Fall: spiritual blindness and the terror inevitable to our condition of contingency, blind as we are to the protective, nurturing, utterly faithful love of our Creator, in whom we live and move and have our being. We instinctively dread the loss of "me," of who I am, my "self"; we dread diminishment, dwindling into nothingness and unimportance.

To a great extent, nature has ways of anaesthetizing this painful awareness. It persists nevertheless and irresistibly urges us to protect with all our might this fragile self. We are told that we must assert our supposed independence, be ourselves the arbiters of what is happiness and glory and go for it. We are desperate to keep control; we watch lest others threaten our rights. In other words, we insist on being our own god. Good, noble, virtuous in all manner of ways, we remain in control. We believe there is no problem in giving generously of the fruits of our vineyard, so long as the vineyard remains our own. And yet it is precisely this jealously guarded

self-possession that must be surrendered. I do not think that
we ourselves can make this absolute surrender. God himself
must do it for us, must wrest us from ourselves. Nevertheless,
if God is to achieve this ultimate triumph, we must do all that
is within our power to help.

"The Son of Man came, not to be served but to serve, and
to give his life as a ransom for many" (Matt. 20:28). Jesus
himself, the humblest of humankind, is the model for what
he is asking of his disciples. Mark's picture of Jesus holding
the child close to him illustrates the point. Jesus is the perfection of spiritual childhood. The stringent *unless* of turning and
becoming as a child in order to enter the kingdom of heaven
is another way of saying that to seek to save one's life in this
world is to lose it. To sacrifice one's life is to gain admittance
into the kingdom of heaven. . . .

. . . It is not things but self that has to be denied.

—*LY*,18–19

WE MUST ACT

*Rachel encourages beginners resolutely to harness their inklings
toward the divine grandeur for which they were made. She
would have them use their created capacities to cultivate openness to the gift of God through what she names "mental labor
and moral effort," or "meditation and asceticism."*

Continually we must hold two strands in our hands and not let
go of one or other if we would get across what a life of deep
faith entails. First, everything is gift and God must do all. Man
can do nothing to bring himself to God. Secondly, man must
not sit with his hands in his lap. He must act. He must do all he
possibly can to grow and to respond to God and without this
preparation God cannot work in man as he wishes. We have to
learn from Jesus what God's will is and try to fulfill it. God isn't
standing by saying: "Now let me see you trying. When I see you
have really tried, I will step in and help." No, this delay of God

is in the nature of things. God is offering himself to me here and now but I cannot receive him. I must have reached a certain level of development before I can begin to do so. New wine cannot be poured into old skins otherwise the skins are spoiled and the wine runs away. God can only come in with his mystical "over-and-above" help when man has reached his limits and can go no further. . . .

I must stress again that all this presupposes generosity. Like the apostles, we must have labored all night and taken nothing before Jesus can fill our nets. The labor is essential. Most of us are not generous enough. The road to life is hard but it is not tortuous or complicated; what is more, it does not cut strange ways for itself. Just because it is God's road it is on this earth, running through our days and years, running through the familiar scenery of our everyday life. To opt out of our ordinary human life is to get off the road. —*TBJ*, 32, 34–35

The appetite for self-gratification must be replaced with an appetite for Christ, for living our human lives as he lived his. Everything has to be seen and judged in the light of Jesus' teaching. The love of Jesus Christ must become our one motivating force.

We come to know Jesus and how he lived by meditation. Two activities dominate the nighting of the ego—meditation and asceticism. The word "meditation" has become a sort of code word with John [of the Cross].

While retaining its specific meaning it serves as a useful shorthand for *all our own efforts* to advance, and this includes asceticism. Our own efforts can never of themselves achieve the essential nighting of the ego, only God can do this; but we have to work hard to make it possible for him to do so. No one will insist more than John that the mountain cannot be scaled by ourselves. Nevertheless he is equally emphatic that unless we do undertake a thorough asceticism we cannot even begin the ascent. This stage of great human effort with what we may here call "ordinary grace" cannot be skipped. . . .

We have one dynamism of choice. That dynamism must be controlled, concentrated, otherwise it ceases to be dynamic and is like a worn out battery driving nothing. If we do not know what we really want, if we vacillate, allowing ourselves to be drawn hither and thither, we become enfeebled and our faculty of choice is weakened. We must decide what we really want and concentrate on that. . . .

. . . The way to grow in love for God, to strengthen motivation, is precisely to keep the will directed, to bring it back when it has strayed. This fidelity opens us to divine influence without which little can be achieved.   —*AL*, 23–24, 43

PERSISTENT PONDERING ON THE SCRIPTURES

The following passages focus squarely on Rachel's counsel regarding meditation. For Rachel, meditation principally means praying with the New Testament, and she shares with us here her own method of scriptural prayer. It also includes praying with liturgical texts and, where possible and appropriate, making use of scriptural commentaries and other theological works. There are two reasons why Rachel sees meditation to be at the heart of spiritual growth. First, if we are called to enter into the life of Jesus, then it is essential that we do whatever is in our power to come to know him. And second, in coming to know him, we are allured into imitation of him; Jesus's self-emptying assent to love gradually becomes more attractive to us than the comfortable familiarity of the ego.

We have here not merely a loving benevolence that showers us with gifts, but a Self-donation, a Self-gift. This is what Jesus reveals. Jesus is himself the very embodiment of the divine gift of Self. His whole life reveals it, but it is on the cross that it shines out with terrible clarity. Jesus, surrendered, poured-out, emptied, is the truest image we have in this life of the heart of the Godhead. Jesus therefore is central to our life in God. If the above is true, which of course it is, incontrovertibly so, then we understand that prayer *is not primarily what we are doing for God but God's Self-offer to us in love; what God works in us*, if we allow him. Our part is to be *there, receiving, assenting and surrendering in response*. We realize too, that our whole life must be involved; the time set aside exclusively to conscious receptivity and response is meaningless unless it is an expression of what we want life itself to be. . . .

Each of us has direct, immediate access to the God of love at every moment. At every moment, each one of us is the object of God's undivided concern. At every moment, divine Love offers Itself to us to purify our hearts of all that is alien to love, everything that is selfish, in order to transform us into Itself. This is what our saints mean by infused contemplation or mystical prayer; not something reserved to a few elect persons but offered to every member of the human race. However, they leave us in no doubt that, if we are to receive this priceless gift or Gift, we must make up our minds to a sustained moral effort and mental labor. Yes, it is offered to all, but very few of us, our saints attest, prepare generously enough to receive it in copious measure.

Evidently, we ourselves, as yet, lack the vibrant faith that is ever attentive, always receptive of God's work of love. We have to labor—the word is not too strong—if this overwhelmingly wonderful truth is to become our very own truth. What is needed is serious, persistent reflection; an ardent search to do whatever is in our power to know Jesus as revealed in the scriptures. "Ardent" does not necessarily imply strong feeling, but genuine desire, constantly renewed and refueled. We become so familiar with the gospel parables and stories; we have listened to them time and time again, so that we think we know and understand them. But have we really "heard" them? Have they resounded in our hearts with power? Have we discerned in these stories the face of the Father which Jesus is always wanting us to see? Have we read them or listened to them with *faith and desire*?

. . . It is incumbent on us to do all we can to deepen faith through the study of scripture and theology. . . . It must be emphasized that this work of the mind is an essential background for what we might call contemplative prayer of Carmel.

. . . Carmel's prayer tends to a certain "passivity." This must be interpreted correctly. In no way is it suggested that a beginner—or anyone else—just sits with folded hands waiting for God to act. No, but once we grasp the "sort of God we have got": self-communicating, ceaselessly working within us to purify and transform us, we will have the only proper attitude: a trustful receptivity. Of course, at the beginning, we cannot have, still less maintain, this faith-filled receptivity, and therefore must help ourselves with reflections and other means. We use them precisely to enable us to affirm and reaffirm our faith in God's presence to us in love and in his work of love in us.

We are not aiming at some sort of achievement—a high state of feeling, for instance, or wonderful insights. We are not out to impress God, still less entertain him! The *means* we use are relatively unimportant, differing from person to person and even for the same person. All the same, this kind of effort of thought in order to be attentive and believing, is indispensable. It opens us to God. We won't be looking for "success"; we won't judge the reality or worth of prayer by what it seems like to us. Of course, if we think of prayer as some sort of holy accomplishment that makes us spiritual; if all the weight is on *my prayer*, then we *do* look for success and satisfaction, and, somewhat complacently assume that we have given God something! But it is *you* God wants, not your spiritual prowess! If we fix our gaze on God or on Jesus (it is all the same), we gradually give up this subtle self-seeking and remain in peace even if prayer is arid, and seems "non-prayer," affording us no satisfaction. No matter what, we must quietly, stubbornly affirm and reaffirm our faith in God's love and self-giving. God has been successful and that is what matters! . . .

The moan "I cannot pray" is non-sense. All it means is that I cannot perform to my satisfaction! *Always* we can put ourselves in Our Lord's presence, a presence unfelt, unseen but *known* by faith; ourselves, just as we are—upset, weary, feeling utterly unspiritual, totally unresponsive to divine things which seem but fairy-tales . . . just as we are, in our poverty and sinfulness; crippled, dumb, and blind, and *stay there*, affirming our faith, humbly, trustingly, under God's loving gaze. We don't wait for the moment when we feel spiritual again, more ready for prayer. Our Lord wants *you*, just as you are—always. —*IP*, 15–18

Certainly methods of prayer will differ according to temperaments and abilities, in the early stages and throughout our whole life, but what is of the utmost importance is persistent pondering on the Scriptures. The New Testament must be the basis of our intellectual knowledge of God and his will for us. Only thus can we rightly interpret every other form of revelation. Our "appetite" for Jesus must be sharp and unabating. . . . The whole of life has to do with the beloved; he is to be found everywhere, in everyone and everything. We question everything by reflection and action. Thinking must of necessity play a vital role, and how essential it is to think rightly of God and his creation. Jesus Christ is our key. Today we have unparalleled opportunity of knowing him, his mind, his values, of viewing God and the world with his vision. Modern scholars have opened up the Scriptures for us as never before. We must avail ourselves of their labors, must enter in and make them our own.

Everything we learn about Jesus must then be translated into living. —*AL*, 24–25

Let me share a favorite method of my own, which has helped many others. It is closely akin to what St. Teresa [of Avila] was suggesting to her novice. Take a story from the Gospels, let us say that of Jesus' encounter with the Samaritan woman (John 4)— John's Gospel is especially helpful for prayer. There you have a wonderful verbal exchange. Read it, recall it, and then believe that you are that person whom Jesus questions and invites you to respond:

> "How can I, a poverty-stricken creature give *You* to drink?" you ask.

"You can," Jesus answers, "by asking me to give it to
you."

"Help me to know who you are; help me to know, to
want, to pay any price for this Gift!"

"You cannot appreciate my Gift. But ask me for it and
you will infallibly receive it."

"Lord, help me! Offer, give me this living water. Draw
me to yourself!"

This faith has to be maintained, no matter what our state of
feeling, no matter how things *seem*. If we think about it we will
realize that there is an implicit but inescapable question at stake
here: "Do I believe in Jesus Christ and in what Jesus reveals of
God, which is nothing other than that God is total, unconditional, Self-communicating love?" So, at prayer we are starkly
confronted with a choice: Do I stake everything on Jesus or do I
choose to rely on my subjective experience?

If the above is true, then our *activity* during a period of personal prayer will consist in maintaining this choice of faith,
employing whatever enables us to do this. The accent is not on
our prayer, our "performance," but on being there, exposed to
God, lovingly eager to receive God and certain that we do so,
regardless of how we feel. God is always at work and God's
work is God.   —*EP*, 177–78

What we must be convinced of is that when we contemplate
Jesus in some incident of his earthly life and commune with him,
it is not make-believe but hard reality. Jesus is not some admired,
loved figure of the past, our heart's hero about whom we fanta-
size, but our living Lord, actually present to us, and always life
giving. He wants us to "meet" him in the incidents of his earthly
life for this is how we get to know him as he is now, and what he
wants of us.   —*LU*, 122

If we are to persevere in constant believing, we need nourishment. The Word is the normal source of nourishment and the

Word above all others is the Jesus-Word: what he did, how he was, what he said. Here—and in the letters of Paul and others— is where we learn what God, the ineffable Beauty and Love to whom we are surrendering ourselves, is truly like. Scripture is not easily understood; we have to approach it with faith and we have to work for it to yield its meaning. There are, of course, excellent books of consummate scholarship to help us in our understanding if we have the time, capacity, and opportunity to avail ourselves of them. But a rich source of theology and prayer at hand for each of us is the Missal. Here we find theology at its purest, theology that is prayed, that *is* prayer. If we were to absorb the contents of the Missal we would need little else. Study the four Eucharistic Prayers, the Prefaces throughout the yearly seasons and the great doxology "Glory to God in the Highest." Look carefully at the Collects, especially the one so easily overlooked, the "Prayer over the Offerings." Then, of course, there are the daily readings from the Old and New Testaments with verses from the psalms: a wealth of prayed theology, the Church's understanding at its purest consisting of treasures old and new.   —*EP*, 8–9

My mind has to supply strong motives for choosing God and his will in concrete instances. Here, I would say, lies our chief weakness. Not sufficient importance is attached to the work the mind must do to set before the heart the motives for choosing what is not immediately and sensibly appealing. This deficiency implies a lack of seriousness and an unwillingness to take trouble. Anyone who really wants God will ceaselessly be thinking of what to do in order to go forward. They will have an eagerness to learn and willingly go to endless trouble. There is a tendency to think that good desires and strong motives will be infused; that if we remain quietly before the Lord in prayer, they will be born in on us; that, when we are tempted and troubled we have only to go before the Lord and we will be changed. It seems to me that a very, very important point is being underplayed.

Understandably there has been a reaction to a mistaken form of meditation which put the whole weight on the intellect as though it were a matter of achieving suitable thoughts of God, intellectual and emotional impressions. What matters is "loving much." Loving means choosing. I'm not "loving much" because I am in thoughtless prayer and with a feeling of love. I am loving much when I pour out my life over the feet of Jesus in his brethren. I have to bring before my mind all sorts of reasons for doing this. I have to get to know God and this will mean getting to know Jesus. But there are other powerful incentives that perhaps have to precede the loving preoccupation with Jesus: consideration of the brevity of our life-span, its mysteriousness, what it is for, its gravity and the appalling danger of wasting it. All day long, if we take the trouble, we can glean in the field of our lives, abundant motives for surrendering ourselves to life's whole meaning—God. We must always have in hand the sword of the spirit which is the word of God with which to combat the temptations to give up the struggle, to fall back into worldliness, to sin in one way or another. We have to be ready with the motives for resisting. By and large this seems badly neglected. We fall, we are sorry, but we don't take any special precaution against the future. What we should do, if we are in earnest, is to have our sword ready in hand for the attack—some thought, some word of remembrance of Jesus which, through deep pondering, has become powerful for us.

There is no question of saying that we must spend our time of prayer in thinking, but only in ensuring we are really directed to God, really choosing him; and at this stage we can do this only insofar as our minds furnish the motives. Needless to say, in all this God's grace is active. He is helping us, yet will never do for us what we can do for ourselves. To insist again, it isn't a case of his refusing to do for us what we can do for ourselves, but that it is this human activity of choosing—a joint operation of mind and heart—which gives growth so that God can do for us what we can't do for ourselves.   —ICE, 23–24

VERY ORDINARY THINGS

Rachel would have us translate everything we learn about Jesus into the language of living—and this translation is what she details through her counsel on asceticism. She perceives the ordinariness of daily life as abounding with opportunities for reorienting our innate grasping for self-fulfillment to an empty-handed surrender to God's love. As we will see in these selections, Rachel's advice takes in both the "unselfing" we initiate ourselves, and that called forth by our relations with our neighbors.

If we were to consult some older manuals dealing with the ascetical life, that is, how we must work in order to overcome our bad habits and acquire virtue, we would probably be given a list of virtues, shown how our Lord himself practiced them in his mortal life, and counsel on how we must imitate him. Likewise we would be given systems of prayer, and rules for organizing our life and governing our conduct. A program would be set before us which we could follow quite meticulously, ticking off one point after another. The great defect of such an approach is that it concentrates on self-perfection. All the attention is on self. We glance at our Lord and imitate him only in order to perfect our behavior and shine before him. It is possible to build a splendid structure of spirituality that has nothing to do with God and his life in us and the approach I have mentioned easily fosters this.

This is not the way to imitate Jesus. A well-worn cliché in pious circles runs: "we must not excuse ourselves when blamed because Jesus was silent before his judges when accused." Is this the significance of our Lord's silence in court? Paul did not think so; he had plenty to say for himself and in no measured terms and he did not hesitate to tell his converts to imitate him as he imitated Christ. Jesus' individual acts cannot be taken one by one and copied. We must get to know the inner attitudes from which all his actions sprang and make these our own. We are not

Jews of ancient Palestine. We have to live according to the mind
of Jesus in our own particular situation.

When we look at Paul's list of virtues which the Christian
must work for we find they are directed away from the self to
others, to life, to reality outside ourselves. There is no question
of watching every word, concentrating on details of behavior;
no fear of self-conceit. There is really only one virtue and that is
love, a great, caring love for others that is patient, kind, compassionate, gentle, humble, long-suffering, tenderly considerate for
the weak, always ready to put others before self. It is a love that
is steadfast and enduring. Perhaps most significantly a love that
"bears all things, believes all things, hopes all things, endures all
things" (1 Cor. 13:7). A love that says "yes" to human life in its
bruising and wounding; that does not escape into a hard shell
but remains quivering and exposed, never embittered, always
seeing beyond appearances to the God who never fails and who
holds his world and all that is in it in his love.   —*TBJ*, 37–38

Let us remind ourselves over and over again that holiness has to
do with very ordinary things: truthfulness, courtesy, kindness,
gentleness, consideration for others, contentment with our lot,
honesty and courage in the face of life, reliability, dutifulness.
Intent, as we think, on the higher reaches of spirituality, we can
overlook the warp and woof of holiness.   —*ICE*, 19

Good people have to be very honest with themselves. They are
not likely to commit sins involving grave matter but unless they
have resolutely set their hearts on God they may well be less
careful in other areas. For instance they are not likely to wrong
their neighbor in a big way, such as fraud. But what about his
reputation? No, not gross calumny, just little insinuations, preg-
nant silences? Committed knowingly these are every bit as serious and as real a "no" to God as flagrant injustices.

The most destructive "no" is that involving full knowledge
and consent. But we can be saying no to wanting to know; we do
not want to see that such and such a practice or habit is contrary

to God's will. This is a prolonged "half-no." If we wanted we could pull it into the light and see it for what it is but we would rather leave it in shadow.

There is of course a blindness inherent in the human condition; we are born blind and must wait for the Lord to give us sight. Growth in spirituality is synonymous with growth in sight. At times we can indeed "see" yet be too weak to integrate in actual living what we understand intellectually. Provided we go on trying, these things in no way prevent God's work in us. They convince us rather of our poverty and need of him. What matters is the resolute *will* to give God here and now what he is asking. That is all we can do and all that matters. Let us do this and we shall grow in understanding and love. We are strengthened and enlightened by every choice of God's will, weakened and blinded to some extent by every refusal. —*AL*, 45

Faith is a fast, it is a refusal to put anything in the place of God, and an acceptance of the consequent sense of deprivation. Faith refuses to seek the sensible assurances our nature craves for, and insists on looking beyond, reaching out to him who cannot be savored in this life. For one who has given his heart to our Lord there is a perennial fast while this life lasts. It is in this context I think that we must look for Christian asceticism. Christian asceticism has its roots in love of Jesus, not in fear of the body and the world at large.

For the fast of faith to be real, for the Christian to maintain a hunger for God, a God who does not satisfy his senses, he must take care not so to encompass himself with the good things of this world that his need for God is not experienced. If his desire for God is genuine, and we must not confuse real desire with a feeling or emotion, then he will want to express it in concrete forms. Outward expressions strengthen the inner disposition. Hunger for God has to be worked for. It is a sustained act of choosing under the influence of grace. The lack of religious emotion, if such there be, may well form part of the fast of faith. Hunger for God is born of faith not of feeling. It is maintained by the exercise of faith. There would be something incongruous in a person insisting that they want God, yet never depriving themselves of anything, always having everything they want when they want it.

Christian austerity aims at freedom and reverence; it ensures that we receive God's gift of pleasure in an ever more personal way. A Christian is dedicated to love and life; love of God and his neighbor, assuring for himself and his neighbor an increasing abundance of life. But we have a murderer in our hearts who would destroy not only ourselves but others also, and we cannot ignore him. Now although we can truly say that a Christian's aim must always be positive, yet to maintain this positive aim he must to some extent adopt a negative one. Thus the negative becomes positive, it is at the service of life. We cannot seek God always and serve our neighbor with a disinterested love until we have looked at ourselves, discerned where we are selfishly seeking ourselves, and then positively denied this self-seeking and worked against it. We can go on blithely thinking we are seeking God and serving our neighbor when all the while we are seeking ourselves and our own satisfaction.

Pleasure and satisfaction accompany every proper human activity. This is God's loving ordinance for us, both to ensure that we fulfill our functions, activate our potentialities and grow, and also to make our earthly life as happy as possible. The trouble is that in our selfishness we seek pleasure at the expense of love and duty. As we have a passion for power so we have a passion for pleasure and satisfaction, whether of the senses or of the spirit. Unless we take careful stock of this, without realizing it we shall become enslaved and at the mercy of our likes and dislikes. Mastery and control do not drop from the skies; we have to discipline ourselves for the sake of love. There must be times when, to ensure our freedom, to ensure that we can say "no" to ourselves, we must deny ourselves some perfectly legitimate pleasure. We have a right to it but for love's sake, to ensure that we can love, we deny ourselves.

Moderate, sustained ascetical practices are of far greater value than spurts of a more drastic kind. Enthusiasm can carry us over the more spectacular feats—night vigils, severe fasts—but enthusiasm doesn't last. It lasts as long as we get a kick out of these things and when the kick goes so does the enthusiasm. It is far better to have established simple, prudent rules for what to eat, how long to sleep and so on, and keep to them. Better moderate, unspectacular discipline than outbursts of sensational penance which do little more than gratify our sense of having done something worthwhile. We are not likely to get much satisfaction from our small but constant acts—on the contrary we are likely to feel ashamed of their inadequacy—but if they are kept up for the love of our Lord, to express in tangible form that we want God to be our heart's love they are of great value and efficacy.

The danger with immoderate penance is that it diverts us from what matters most, the continual waiting on God to see what he wants of us: fidelity in this duty, kindness to that person we don't want to be kind to, application to the work we are set when we want a change, and so on. To undertake special acts of penance can give us the illusory sense that we are generous people, that God matters a lot to us, when all the time we are struggling to keep him and his demands out of earshot.

At the beginning of our life for God we have to be tougher on ourselves, especially if we have indulged ourselves and had everything pretty much as we want it. We are not going to get out of this bad habit of self-indulgence without a struggle and our earnestness in this will be proof of the genuineness of our desire to live for God. When we have acquired a measure of control then we can allow ourselves greater freedom. If our hearts belonged wholly to God we could be completely free and happy in the use of everything God has given us, but until we are we have to watch jealously lest craving for our own pleasure blunts our earnestness in seeking God.

This watchfulness over the desire for pleasure and satisfaction must extend to spiritual things as well. Bodily indulgence can

humiliate us but spiritual indulgence foments pride. We may, at
times, derive immense satisfaction from our spiritual duties, at
other times not. Or there may be some spiritual activities which
give us satisfaction and others that don't. For instance, we may
get much more satisfaction attending a shared prayer session
than we do from Mass. What matters is that we never allow
such satisfaction to become a motive force. It can do so without
our realizing it. We are not asked to reject the delight we might
feel in our devotional activities, of course not, but we must not
give this delight a significance it has not got. Because we get a
greater sense of God's presence at a prayer meeting than at Mass
or in silent prayer, it does not mean that God is in fact more for
us in the prayer meeting and that we are justified in opting for
that form of spiritual activity rather than for those which give no
satisfaction. Perseverance in spiritual duties whether pleasurable
or not is of supreme importance. To take up this or that because
it pleases, because it is interesting, and to drop it when the interest goes; to pray when we feel like it and not when we don't, is
to make a farce of prayer and to use God for our self-indulgence.

The most valuable form of asceticism, because it is the actual
exercise of love, is the patient acceptance of the hardships and
sufferings of life. For every good, responsible person there is a
large measure of suffering which he takes in his stride, hardly
adverting to it—it is part of life. Nevertheless it is just this hidden cross, patiently shouldered day after day, that gradually
wears down selfishness. It is the more precious in that it is hidden even from ourselves and does not flatter our pride.

—*TBJ*, 70–74

A little honest reflection shows us that naturally we are our
own horizon, the most important person in the universe. Our
attention and energy are largely employed in looking after ourselves in one way or another. Education, culture, pressures of
our social milieu impose a certain altruism but it is skin deep.
All of us recognize some obligations to others, duties to be done,
sacrifices to be made, but it largely lies within our own decision

as to where we draw the line. We assume unquestionably that we have the right to be treated justly, allowed independence, be consulted, recognized, appreciated. We are very, very important to ourselves and we demand that others recognize this importance. Of course often we do not get what we consider just treatment, adequate recognition, and this makes us angry and bitter. All sorts of devices will be employed even unconsciously to have our importance acknowledged. Often these devices are dishonest and unfair to our neighbor but we choose not to advert to the fact.

John [of the Cross] says if you want God, if you want to begin the ascent of the mountain, then you have to make a decision against self-importance. You have to remove yourself from the center-stage, see yourself as a member of a family, a community which you must serve. This is what Jesus taught and Paul after him. Never think yourself more important than others, never put yourself before them. John expresses it typically in hyperbolic language: do things which bring you into contempt and want others to do likewise. Speak disparagingly of yourself and contrive that others do so too. Think humbly and contemptuously of yourself and want others to do so as well. What odious creatures we should be were we to carry out these injunctions literally! Can we see what he is hinting at in the above? Instead of the words "contemptuously," "disparagingly," substitute "little of." Think little of yourself and be happy that others do not consider you very important. Have a lowly opinion of yourself, not in the sense of unhealthy self-denigration but in that you do not consider yourself the pivot of the universe. Keep correcting in the silence of your heart the contrary natural attitude. Keep reminding yourself that others are more important than you are, that their well-being is more than the satisfaction of your ego. Let your actions conform to this truth. Do not demand that circumstances change to fit you, do not labor to control events for your own benefit. See yourself as the servant of others.

Such a willingness to forget the ego, to lose sight of it, calls for firm faith in God's love. Each of us is utterly important to

God; we can afford to relax a bit and let him look after our little selves. We tend to think that unless we take care of "number one" nobody will. Faith tells us there is one who never takes his eyes off us, so much so that not a hair of our head is lost. . . .

The stress on unimportance in no way overlooks the God-given need within each of us to be loved and accepted. It is surely *God's* will that his children meet with such always, finding in this a reflection of his own love and acceptance. In so far as it depends on us we must give these to all we encounter. However the fact remains that we are limited, fallible, sinful, blind, and so often we suffer from one another, feeling we are overlooked, undervalued. We must be prepared to be so and maintain peace of heart. We cannot accept and love others completely until we are free of our ego and it is the weaknesses, limitations, even downright malice of others that, if we but accept, exorcises this tyrant.   —*AL*, 37–39, 42

Temperaments differ widely but even the most sanguine and even-tempered among us suffer negative moods from time to time, and when they are on us our instinct is to "have" them, to "sit in them," to curl up inside ourselves and, at least for a time, regard ourselves as the most important person in the world. Nothing and no one matters, only unhappy me! Such is our natural instinct.

Feeling bad-tempered, frustrated, unhappy, we make others aware of it. We let off our irritation and our disgruntlement, spread gloom in the office, dampen the atmosphere of a parish meeting, a family gathering. It may not occur to us that this is unchristian behavior, deeply uncharitable and, at bottom, a denial of Jesus. Identifying with these negative feelings is, here and now, a refusal to believe in his love. It is to ignore his passionate longing that we should love one another and so bear witness to the world that God is love. Rather, we are adding to the world's unhappiness and despair.

It is not a small fault to let off our disgruntlements, complaints and personal misery indiscriminately on other people who, for all we know, are already burdened. "Bear one another's burdens," do not add to them. We are Christians and such behavior is a scandal. "See how these Christians love one another." Where is our witness?

Loyal love refuses to be miserable and self-pitying, nursing resentments and little hurts. These things must be seen as temptations to sin and firmly rejected. We feel depressed, sad. We have a choice: stay self-absorbed in the dark, unhappy mood, or, while fully recognizing the mood, we can choose not to identify with it, refuse to be self-absorbed.

If we pray and live our Christian lives faithfully, feeding on all that God has done for us and offers to us in Jesus, then we can choose to "deny self," deny ourselves the "luxury" of self-pity and affirm our blessedness.

Each of us has one life to live in this world and this life has eternal consequences, for myself and for all other people. If only we could realize how precious, how loaded with consequences is each hour of this life! How many treasures we let fall, how much gold we tread underfoot, opportunities for growing in love of God, of "storing up treasure in Heaven," disregarded, thrown away!

It is of the deepest concern to our loving Creator that we, so gently favored, be thoroughly Christian. Gloominess, bad temper and moroseness are totally out of place among us. Though we may not be able to throw off a feeling of sadness, we must assume a quiet, unobtrusive cheerfulness. A feeling of grief, sadness, any painful emotion that cannot be dispelled, is an affliction that, borne unselfishly, can be deeply purifying.

Loyal love can smile through tears and the sobbing of a broken heart will be free of bitterness. St. Thérèse of Lisieux, intent on garnering every detail of her life as a sacrificial offering "for souls," declared that she was happy in times of unhappiness as these, too, could be offered to Our Lord. Even when we are quite alone and there is no question of our distressing others, Our Lord would ask us to refuse to dwell on, in any way to identify with, our negative moods.

As already remarked, this particular, unspectacular denying of self is of untold value in God's eyes, enabling him to give himself to us in growing measure. Our inner afflictions become a real sharing in our Savior's passion. If only every one of his Christian people paid full attention to this interior asceticism that is at hand day by day, what benefits would accrue for the Church and the world so in need of the presence of holiness! . . .

. . . We cannot know in this life how that hidden, brave asceticism opens our sad world for God's love to flow in.

—*SH*, 10–11

5

Receiving the Gift of God

Jesus was so given, so surrendered, so emptied out, that
he was like a hollow shell in which the roar of the ocean
could be heard. He was an emptiness in which the Father
could fully express his own self-giving being. We have to
be living embodiments of Jesus, as he is of the Father.
                                                    —OF, 40–41

We have arrived at Rachel's rich and extensive wisdom on
receiving the gift of God's outpoured love directly into the fabric
of our being. Here, what was previously anticipated begins to
be realized. This is the second stage in the journey of spiritual
transformation; it is the beginning and development of the mys-
tical life. We know that we receive the inundation of God's love
through union with the self-emptying Jesus. Thus, contrary to
popular expectations and much spiritual writing, the mystical
life means descending into resolute empty-handed trust in God's
love in the midst of our human fragility and poverty rather than
ascending to glorious heights of religious fervor.

Much of what Rachel presents in the following selections is
the fruit of her lifelong commitment to extracting the shining
Gospel core from the mystical doctrines of St. Teresa of Avila
and St. John of the Cross. She helps us to realize that mysti-
cism is not the privileged domain of those living in Carmelite
monasteries, or, at the very least, religious specialists. Rather, the
mystical life, life lived in the kenotic Jesus, is the flowering of our

baptism and has everything to do with ordinary, daily decisions for God and others, and against self-satisfaction.

GOING BACKWARD

This first set of selections conveys Rachel's general thought on how the dawning of the mystical life impacts our lived experience. While, in our hidden depths, we are being drawn into union with the living God, it seems to us that we are going backward. As we are taken down the mountain of egocentricity and into Jesus's self-emptying, what fills our vision is the towering vanity of what we thought was our spiritual security.

God does not answer man's expectations, the expectation of pride, of flesh and blood, not of the Spirit of God who wills all that is best for man. God does not do what man expects him to do, does not approach him in the form he wants, which at the deepest level means that God, far from boosting man and making him feel grand, does exactly the opposite. The effect of God drawing close to us always means that what Isaiah said of the suffering servant becomes true for us. In a very deep way we have to sacrifice that which seems to make us man, what we think of as a beautiful spirituality; we have to be changed in a way that *seems* to make us less, not more human. There is nothing here naturally attractive to man; rather, his instinct must be to turn away in revulsion. This, in practice, in hard reality, is what it means to embrace Jesus crucified, and embracing him, embrace he who sent him and whose revelation he is. . . .

Our spiritual achievement is our most precious treasure. It has to go. "For his sake," cries one who understood this, "I have suffered the loss of all things and count them as refuse, in order that I may gain Christ and be found in him not having a righteousness of my own, based on law, but that which is through faith in Christ" (Phil. 4:8–9). Now we can only begin to see the shabbiness of all we have done and do when God shows it to us. But what matters is that we recognize that it is God who is showing it to us and gladly let it go. The ideas we had formed of God, our working plan of him, so to speak, is destroyed. "Our" God disappears. It is only when he does disappear that we can meet the true God, who is mystery, and who leaves us baffled, wretched, bitterly aware of our lack of goodness. We thought we were doing well, we thought we were virtuous, we thought we were spiritual and look at us now, after all these years . . . Our minds wander at prayer, we have no light, no comforting, reassuring feelings which tell us that everything is well with us and that God is pleased. On the contrary we feel the opposite. Instead of going forward—our own idea of going forward—we seem to be going backwards. We are humbled to the dust and in danger of packing up unless we know what trust in God means. And, of course, since this painful condition is the effect of God's drawing near, faith and trust are infused. We are able to trust him.   —*TBJ*, 24–25, 93

His presence to us in love has a twofold simultaneous effect— that of purifying and transforming. God does not purify us through some agent other than himself and then when we are purified come to us and transform us. His presence *is* our purifi- cation. The living flame, God himself invades us, but that which is supreme bliss is first experienced as purgation for it destroys and consumes in us all that is alien to him. . . .

The image "dark night" clearly suggests the aspect of purifi- cation as it is experienced by us, but we must never forget that transformation (or we could equally well say "becoming") is in exact proportion to purification. In the degree that fire dries out moisture it transforms the matter into fire itself. The divine gaze of love, even as it imprints its own likeness on us reveals most painfully our own swarthiness. . . .

. . . Any one who has experience of homeopathic healing will have an excellent image of what is happening. The progress of a homeopathic cure can be dramatic. Far from seeming better the patient throws up alarming symptoms: rash, fever, boils, sickness, headaches; as the body rids itself of deep-seated toxins. All the

poisons absorbed through life are gradually rejected. It is a drastic but thorough-going treatment. In between the bouts of violent cleansing the patient knows periods of delightful well-being
and imagines he is fully healed, only to be submerged again in
another intense purgation. The dark night bears a resemblance
to this. The purgation continues until everything that is alien to
God is destroyed. . . .

. . . Nothing can be said of the heart of the experience, the
contact with the divine reality; this must, of its nature, escape
detection. All that can be described are the effects and among
these we must discern what are the essential effects and what
circumstantial and ambiguous. The essential effects are three: a
painful awareness of sinfulness, lack of satisfaction in meditation (that is, "aridity"), and growth in goodness.   —AL, 49–51

PAINFUL KNOWLEDGE OF SELF

*We saw at the end of the previous section that our general feel-
ing of going backward as God draws close to us can be discussed under three aspects. Here, Rachel considers the first:
painful self-knowledge. As the divine light irradiates our depths,
we discover, to our dismay, the extent of our ego-possession and
the shabbiness of our self-made virtue. The first selection from*
Guidelines for Mystical Prayer *is an excerpt from a letter to
Rachel from her dear spiritual friend.*

When God, all-love, love that in its human expression sheds its
last drop of blood for us, draws close, the ego can have no part
with him, it is the dead opposite of such self-giving love. The ego
is then shown up for what it is in its distortion and ugliness. In
its own estimation and in the estimation of other egotisms it had
seemed fine enough. Now it is beginning to be unmasked and
revealed as it is. We have a choice—to accept this unmasking,
consent that the ego should die and so have part with the humble
Lord, or turn away our face from him and reinstate our threatened dignity. We cannot have him *and* our pride and satisfaction.
                                                          —AL, 58–59

Don't you see too that, if you are seeing Jesus, if the Holy One
enfolds you then you are bound to feel with appalling pain that
you are sinful. "Depart from me for I am a sinful man." You
could never see this before. Oh, I know we think we do, we
think we know we are sinful and wretched and so on but we
don't. It is only when Jesus comes to us in this sort of way that
we see it and it is very, very hard to bear until we grasp the full
significance of it and then it becomes our joy. It is really this, a
fundamental choice: will I let Jesus be my holiness and stand
in the blazing truth, or will I insist on having a holiness of my
own—to offer him, of course, to be pleasing in his eyes? The
whole essence of the Christian demand is to let God be our God
and refuse to be God to ourselves. And this is what you are
being faced with in a very deep way now. You can say "no" and
it won't seem a "no," it may seem the utmost generosity. You
could kill yourself with penances and good works, you could
make sure that not one iota of the law is unfulfilled, you could
guard against any possible failing and make quite sure you have
no need of a savior, of a Jesus. You could present yourself before
him a worthy bride. Isn't that what we are trying to do secretly?
And can you see what I am trying to say, the orientation we must
make? It consists fundamentally in a total acceptance of the bitter experience of our poverty and an obstinate refusal to evade
it; to accept to stand, in very deed not just in pious imagination,
stripped before the living God, our leprosy laid bare, crippled in
limb, blind, deaf, dumb—a living need. How few will live thus
and let him be their savior, their life, their light, their food and
drink. We want to feel holy, to feel we are really spiritual with
deep understanding and insight, pure and noble of heart. "You
alone are the holy one" is the cry of truth and happy those for
whom it is the truth they live by. This is what is being asked of
you now, my dear. Can you accept it?   —*GMP*, 88–89

An awareness of our sinfulness is part of holiness; you simply
cannot have holiness without it for it is the inevitable effect of

God's closeness. This is why true sorrow for sin is never morbid, depressed; for it carries with it the certainty of forgiveness.

—OF, 51

It is significant that when St. John of the Cross begins to treat of the mystical action of God he turns our attention to what are known as the capital sins. He wants to convince us of our innate sinfulness so that we may approach God with humility and self-distrust. He tells us that the habits of sin are so deeply rooted that only God can destroy them. We must let him. The mystical action of God gradually reveals these tenacious sinful habits. We must accept the painful knowledge of self and look to God alone for healing.

Too easily spiritual people think they are beyond the stage of considering the capital vices, quite overlooking the tenacious, all-pervading, profound nature of their hold upon us. They are perversions of God-given tendencies and are the direct and terrible consequence of original sin. In their gross form they are less harmful simply because their grossness offends our human dignity. It is their subtle ramifications which are deadly. More harmful than any single, even grave, fault are attitudes we have adopted, stands we take without realizing their sinfulness. . .

Pride and Sloth

Pride and sloth together form the tap root from which the other sins branch out. They pervade them all. Respectively they pervert two complementary aspects of reality, that we are very small before the great God, his creatures, but on the other hand, we are made in his image and therefore of infinite value. He loves us and this is our value.

If we think sloth is just laziness, we have minimized it out of all recognition. It can be the most energetic who are the most slothful. Sloth is a distortion of the true unimportance that all men must feel before their maker, and its reaction is to elude right responsibility. I feel that the total demands and promises of God are not for me and therefore do not hold myself responsible in failing to meet them. Each of us has a human responsibility sharpened and colored for each of us by special vocation. Sloth evades this often by the fever of its own activity. Sloth is very readily "satisfied," readily says to itself that I keep the Rule, am a faithful nun, am helpful to others, undertake work cheerfully, what else is expected? All this gives no right whatever to say enough, "I am giving you enough, Lord." Of course we would never articulate this even to ourselves but deeds speak louder than words. The total giving of love is too much for it, it will not, when we really get down to it, take the trouble. There are no holidays, no loopholes in love, no private little areas for myself. Sloth wants all these, though under different names. That is why activity, whether physical or intellectual, can give the slothful such comfort. It blocks out the demands of love, which always looks not to what we do but why.

Pride distorts the nature of our true value. We can follow all the traditional paths of humility and still the citadel of pride remains unshaken. Pride refuses to accept its poverty. The proud cannot bring themselves to hold out empty hands to God, they insist on offering virtues, good works, self denials, anything in order not to have nothing. They want to be beautiful for him from their own resources, whereas we are beautiful only because God looks on us and makes us beautiful. This is repugnant to pride. God cannot give himself to us unless our hands are empty to receive him. The deepest reason why so few of us are saints is because we will not let God love us. To be loved means a naked, defenseless surrender to all God is. It means a glad acceptance of our nothingness, a look fixed only on the God who gives, taking no account of the nothing to whom the gift is made. To lose ourselves like this is the most radical of despoliations because the last shred of self-importance is discarded. The very words and acts of humility can be a barricade of well-nigh infinite subtlety. Jesus came to us precisely to break down the bars, something we could never have done ourselves. Yet we cannot live the life of Jesus unless we consent to leave our own pitiful lives, and this is what pride finds unendurable. Striving for "perfection" is the

most disastrous of the mistakes good people fall into. It feeds the
very vice it intends to destroy. Most fervent souls are prepared to
give God any mortal thing, work themselves to death, anything
except the one thing he wants, total trust: anything but surrender into this loving hands. "You must become as little children,"
whose one virtue is that they know they are unimportant.

—*GMP*, 75, 82–84

There is, I think, a particular aspect of pain that gets neglected
in that it is deemed too mean, shameful even, to form part of
what we are happy to offer to God. It is an incommunicable
pain having to do just with me being me and a me I do not
like. Instinctively we contrast this unclaimed pain with "real"
suffering: bereavement, oppression, torture, hunger, imprison-
ment, illness, and so forth and we feel still more ashamed and
self-despising. Some of us know this about themselves but some,
I think, do not and therefore this particular pain, so precious, I
believe, in God's eyes, is not exposed to him and so it blocks our
capacity for wholehearted love; we are that much less a person.
The pain may be precisely the inability to accept self. Let us take
every aspect of our human experience and spread it out to God
without fear, without shame.   —*QUD*, 8

A SENSE OF ARIDITY

*The second inevitable impact on our lived experience of God's
mystical presence in our inner being is spiritual aridity. As we are
incorporated by the Spirit into Jesus's communion of love with
the Father, the spiritual nourishment we formerly supplied ourselves in prayer through our own resources ceases to satisfy us.
We are left feeling blank and rootless during our times of prayer.*

In the mystical encounter, however fleeting, the deep self has had
a glimpse of Reality itself and cannot but spurn imitation. The
moment passes but in some way the self can never forget this
glimpse and its experience is colored by it. One of the effects is
what we normally call aridity. The growing spiritual being within

is now impatient of the coarse food the mind supplies. Hence a sense of aridity, distaste. Spurned by the inner self, useless, empty, the ordinary channels of communication echo hollowly with every kind of noise and disturbance while the choosing self feeds secretly on divine food. . . .

What will an hour of prayer be like when our mind can give us nothing to use to "put myself in the presence of God," to contemplate him? Naturally, by sheer instinct, by all we are, we reach out to God in thought and the follow-up of desire. There is no other way for us but that. Let us say we have been in earnest, have really tried in every way we can think of to do what God asks and that we go to prayer with as pure a motive as possible—to want God and him alone. But when we go to prayer there is nothing there. Of course we can think thoughts, we could take a book and help ourselves to find good thoughts to move our will to want God, but these thoughts are empty, dead as dodos. How then do we "get in touch with God"? How are we to think of him? Where is he? Is he anywhere? Here we are, a solid block of flesh, kneeling or sitting in church or somewhere else. Everything is solid and real around us—the walls, the sound of life outside, voices, cars. That is our world, in a short time we will be back in it again. What is real? How unreal, insubstantial, seems the notion of God and prayer to him. Nothing, nothing whatever to assure us of his presence, of the value of what we are doing. This is when so many give up or, if they don't give up completely, retreat from where they are, determining to make prayer more alive, more interesting, more obviously the "real thing." They may succeed in convincing themselves that now, at last, they have something—this is the real thing! They are mistaken. The only way forward is into mystery which is extremely painful. We crave for what is suited to us, what we can understand, can encompass, for what gives us a sense of security and worthwhileness. The mystery which is God gives us none of these things on the level at which we want them. We are being summoned to the espousals of the cross.   —*ICE*, 60, 62–63

Faith is being freed from the limitations to which it was subject on the first island when the mind had to search for and examine revealed truth. Now faith supplies the content. It is God himself, in himself not an image, that is known and loved though in darkness. This knowledge is not "outside" us but of our substance. The mysteries of Jesus formerly seen from outside and consciously made the principles by which one must guide one's life, are now our own life; we are living the mysteries of Jesus—progressively of course. We may be quite unable, at least at times, to look in any meaningful way upon these mysteries simply because they have become our life. For instance, we may assist at Mass with deep aridity, unable to "enter into it," but our life is the Mass, an ever-growing surrender with Jesus to the Father. Likewise the Trinity is no abstract notion but living truth. We are in the Trinitarian stream—to the Father in Jesus through the Spirit. The mystery of suffering, the folly of the cross is ours, and thus with other truths. At times our mind may be able to grope after what we understand in an incomprehensible way, in order to give of our light to others, but as often as not this conceptualization will leave us completely arid. We may know we are feeding others but feel starved ourself.

—*GMP*, 93

It seems we are asked to let prayer disappear, surrender our "spiritual life," have no control over it. Yes, this is what must happen. We have to give full space to the Spirit awaking within us, uttering his secret inarticulate prayer. This is true prayer. Even the best spiritual education cannot "do it for us." Each of us must choose to trust not our own subjectivity but the God of all goodness and fidelity as revealed in Jesus; he who has sworn by his own eternal being that we are his dearly beloved and that he is our own God who will bring us to perfect fulfillment in himself. In all other areas of our human existence we can try to gain control, manage for ourselves; in this we learn the opposite, learn to let go, let another take over, one we cannot see, feel, or taste.   —*AL*, 57

MYSTICAL SUFFERING

Much wisdom is contained in this short section. "Mystical suf-
fering" is the pain we've been considering so far; it is the distress
we experience as what we thought was our security crumbles—
even though all the while our true security, life in Jesus, is taking
root in our depths. Rachel's insight here is that while the top-
pling of the ego must be absolute, the suffering it brings need
not be out of the ordinary. Indeed, this suffering is likely to be
unromantically embedded in the natural, normal progress of life.
We glimpse Rachel's own experience here, under the guise of
"Petra."

[T]he heart must be totally purified of egotism if we are to receive
God fully—"annihilated" is not too strong a term. Although we
have to do all we can to deny our egotism wherever we meet it,
its overthrow can only be a divine work and it takes place in
God's coming to us and our welcoming him. This is the essence
of the night understood as purgation. It is a burning away of
egotism, the death of the "old man" and the substitution of the
divinely human life, Jesus-life, for the sinful human life. What it
feels like will vary enormously from person to person.

We can use the homely image of laundering. Essentially the
purification of washing is the same, but different materials need
different treatment. A linen tablecloth will "experience" a most
intense form of washing: boiling water, vigorous pummeling in
the machine, thorough wringing out and hanging up exposed to
wind and sun. An angora jersey is immersed in warm soft-soap
water, gently swished, not wrung but patted tenderly and laid
out in a protected place to dry. A camel-hair coat will be sent
to the dry cleaners for progressive attention; it will know nothing of water or washing machine. Though all three are cleansed,
purified, the experience of each differs considerably. We could
say the linen is cleansed in a dramatic way with passionate
intensity; the wool with slowness and gentleness; the camel-hair
with aridity and in a manner hard to associate with washing. . . .

. . . An attempt to assess the reality and depth of divine purgation by the kind and intensity of suffering is erroneous. What we
must hold on to is that God's purifying action is *always* effective
in destroying *egotism*. This is the real affliction whereas what we
do almost always inflates the ego. True affliction deprives us of
every vestige of self-complacency. It is often low-keyed, miserable, something we are ashamed to call suffering. . . .

God alone knows the inmost personal being and how it must
be purified, he can be relied on. But means have infinite varia-
tions. Experience of his work in others leaves us amazed, awe-
struck over and over again at the subtlety of his ways. He knows
just where to put his finger, knows the inmost fibers and just
where the disease has grip. We can never see this beforehand for
ourselves. We see it maybe when it actually happens, either in
ourselves or others. We may have prayed with deep earnestness
for God to purify us, to accomplish his work at whatever cost;
and then something will come about, perhaps trivial in nature,
that touches our most vulnerable spot, and we find ourselves
saying, "anything but *this*"; yet *this* is our tenacious ego.

—*AL*, 107–8, 109, 112

[W]e must insist that it is a mistake to think that extreme suffering—using that word in its usual sense, covering the experiences
we generally have in mind—is essential to total union with God.
What is essential is the death of the ego, because this is the reverse
side of our union with God. The inescapable (if we would attain
this union) and truly mystical suffering is the mortal wounding
of the ego, and I could well imagine this taking place, perhaps
more effectively, where great suffering, in the ordinary sense, is
absent. The real thing is likely to operate in an unobtrusive way,
hidden behind what seem purely natural factors. . . .

. . . Did [Petra] experience more intense trials toward the end?
Her answer was reserved. In one sense the suffering was less
because her trust in God had grown. In another greater, because
within the space of two years she was called upon to relinquish
her last toe-holds on human happiness and security. . . .

No one could say that these troubles, of themselves, were worth writing home about. They belong to the common lot. But Petra saw God in them—ah, not in a way that "sublimated" them, no, they were experienced in their earthy bitterness—but she understood that this is how he comes. He asked her to abandon the last shreds of security, shreds that gave her some sort of meaning; asked her to look only to him for meaning and fulfillment. —*GMP*, 107, 110, 113–14

THE WISDOM OF THE CRUCIFIED ONE

The third inevitable impact on our lived experience of the dawning of the mystical life in our depths is variously named. In essence, it is the divine enablement to sustain the undoing of the ego. As we are taken by the Spirit into the mind and heart of the kenotic Jesus we are enabled to accept the backward way we seem to be traveling, knowing with a knowledge that doesn't belong to the ego that such is the way to true fulfillment.

A third effect of the mystical grace is seen in the quality of life. This is hard to assess, and the older I get the more I realize that discernment of spirits is a gift and it is rare. All of us can estimate ordinary virtue, but when it comes to something more subtle than that, few can discern it. What I have in mind is an element, very diminutive perhaps, of that divine wisdom which baffles human wisdom, the folly of the cross. This is the most certain of all the signs of the mystical. There is a growing insight. We are beginning to see God where we never thought he was, in what upsets our preconceived ideas of God, of what he does and what his drawing near will be like. We shall begin to listen to God, to what he is asking here and now, and this may run counter to what we have been conditioned to expect. It may set us at odds with the milieu in which we live. The tendency to criticize others will disappear and our heart will become kind and compassionate. It won't just be a question of doing things for others, serving them—this need not go beyond the bounds of "virtue," of "the law"—but a true preferring of others to self in all things. In general there will be a growing willingness to accept on every level, a sense of unimportance, to become as small as a child. To draw near to God is to abandon every ambition, and when we have abandoned earthly ones we grasp at spiritual ones. The ego must begin to die. Only God's mystical action can bring this about.

—*GMP*, 34

It is the wisdom of the crucified One—sheer folly, scandalous!—a wisdom that perceives divine love and love's action where natural wisdom would deride or shrink back in disgust. Divine wisdom gently coaxes us to submit to being purified of self, to being comforted in our helplessness and poverty; it persuades us to surrender control, and to abandon ourselves blindly to love.

—*EP*, 80

Flesh and blood do not reveal these things, nor enable us to respond. There is a force, a Spirit within, that prompts, urges, enables us to ignore our own natural estimation of how things stand, and choose, instead, to believe. Nothing runs so counter to nature as the experience of our spiritual poverty, and a practical love for it such as this can only be the work of the Holy Spirit, the Spirit of Jesus. Do we not recognize the truth of Scripture that, in spite of everything that is "against us," we are grounded in an invincible hope "because the love of God has been poured into our hearts by the Holy Spirit who has been given to us" (Rom. 5:5). We are being led, not by nature, but by the Spirit, for we are indeed God's children and the Spirit inspires our spirit to cry out in confidence: "Father, my dear Father" (cf. Rom. 8:14–16). It is the Spirit who continually upholds our natural weakness with divine strength; who is always praying deep within us even when our hearts seem mute, uttering our own most authentic desires, desires that we hardly know we have.   —*EP*, 63

Faith is not so much a grasp of truths of faith and assent to them, though this is part of it; faith is a "knowing" not "about God" but a knowing God—an obscure, secret knowledge which is the source of one's living. It is not something felt, it is not a clarity of mind or a sense of firmness of will in assent; it is a "being held" which makes us hold on in darkness and bewilderment, when commonsense, all that we ordinarily mean by experience, draws a blank. Faith holds us within, in our inmost citadel, without rhyme or reason, it seems.   —*ICE*, 64

CHOOSE TO TRUST

Each of the passages in the following long section is a variation on a theme that is central to Rachel's thought on receiving the gift of God: the choice to trust. This is a sharing in Jesus's trusting, empty-handed "Yes" to God's total self-gift. We are enabled to make this choice to trust; as we have seen, as God takes over in our depths, the impulse to accept the ego's transformation into Jesus's receptivity to God's love is infused into the fabric of our lived experience.

For Rachel, we incarnate Jesus's surrender to the Father by choosing to trust in God's outpoured love through every encounter with the poverty of our human condition. In the selections below, she contemplates this trust at work as we respond to the revelations of our weakness and sinfulness with humble confidence in God's love; she also considers the terrible reverse of such humility: self-trust. We see trust at work in the cultivation of an "active passivity" in prayer, where our "blankness" is accepted and nurtured as pure capacity for God's unseen and unfelt outpouring of love. And trust is at work as we accept our ultimate inability to control the circumstances of our life and chose to stand vulnerable before people and events in all their otherness, receptive to the love God mediates through them.

Nothing so glorifies God, so pleases him as our trust. I know many people who say simply and sincerely that they love God and their lives prove that this is not mere sentiment. For myself, I have never been able to say it. It has seemed presumptuous for me to do so, claiming a sort of proportionality between God and

me. Most certainly, I have wanted to love him and it has been
and is my belief, my hope, and my confidence that, when his
work in me is complete, I will love him because I will love with
the heart of Christ.

It is hard, at least for me, to detach the word "love" from
feeling and in my case feelings of love, generally speaking, have
been absent. Still I maintain that trust includes everything and is
infinitely pleasing to God. It *is* love in that it is yearning desire
for what the heart lacks, coupled with confidence that its desire
will be fulfilled. It is adoration and pure worship, for it acknowl-
edges God for what he is, infinite fidelity and love. It is a practical avowal that we have absolutely nothing as of ourselves, that
everything, everything, whatsoever it may be, is all from him, is
all gift. It is affirming the absoluteness of God and his absolute
claim on the human heart.

Trust takes God at his word, trusting that word beyond every
subjective emotion and experience, beyond everything that seems
to contradict it, against all temptation from within or without.

Trust is implicit thanksgiving. "We give you thanks for your
great glory," is the cry of the trusting heart. The trust I mean is
inseparable from faith and hope. It is not just intellectual assent
to a statement of faith, it is a surrender of self to God. It is the
human answer to God's revelation of himself, to his utter reliability and his steadfast loving kindness toward us. It is the answer
God has longed for down the ages and has so rarely received.
One has given it and in our name: Jesus, the great "Amen" (Rev.
3:14; cf. 2 Cor. 1:19–20).

"Truly I say to you, unless you turn and become like children,
you will never enter the kingdom of heaven" (Matt. 18:3). Jesus
was always the child. A child is totally dependent on its parents
for simply everything. Instinctively it knows it is unimportant,
knows it is helpless and without resources of any kind; and,
again instinctively, is utterly sure that, preciously loved as it is, it
will be cared for. Jesus is telling us that we must *choose* to trust
the Father with the same absolute, unquestioning trust a child
has by instinct in its parents. To do this consistently throughout

our life is the hardest thing possible. "Narrow is the gate and strait the way that leads to life and few there are that find it" (Matt. 7:14). We must "strive" to enter by this narrow gate (cf. Luke 13:24). Jesus is this narrow gate, Jesus in his lowly humanity, in his full acceptance of that humanity in its weakness, its suffering and its mortality. . . .

He is our pioneer, our leader in faith and trust and it is from his surrender that we draw strength to do what of ourselves we cannot do. —*LU*, 143–47

We have no holiness, goodness or wisdom of our own. So to be made consciously aware that we are spiritually inadequate, faulty, wretched—that we fail and sin—is a precious grace.

Pride would make us angry with ourselves, or discouraged. Or on the other hand it might come into play further back and not allow us to become aware of our failings. It would provide us with the knack of sweeping them under the carpet, so we didn't have to face them.

Christian humility quietly faces up to all this without anger or discouragement. It calls to mind that there is One who always did his Father's will; who offers the Father perfect love and worship. And this One is the Father's gift to us.

From the shelter of the Son's heart we go on trying, with him, to do always what pleases the Father; but at the same time never wanting to feel we are becoming holy and good, without spot or wrinkle.

Never are we more truly in Christ Jesus than when, deeply conscious of our sinfulness, we peacefully rest in the heart of our Redeemer—the Risen One. —*LL*, 22–23

[T]here are only two things we can give God: trust and acceptance of poverty.

Confidence, not love, is basic. Love is the summit, and confidence leads to love. I am sure it is confidence we need to develop and pay most attention to; all the rest will flow from it. We have to take God at his word, "Ask and you will receive, seek and you shall find."

We really have to believe that God wants to give us nothing less than himself, is only waiting to pour himself into us. We have to take him at his word as he reveals himself in the Gospels—the friend of sinners, one who throws his arms around the wayward, ungrateful son and kisses him in all his filthy rags. This is God.

Does our disposition of soul respond to this God or have we formed our own image of him projected from human experience? The biggest obstacle to trust seems to be a wrong idea of God, a projection of self-image. We feel unlovable therefore God cannot love us, or so we think. By faith we know this is nonsense, but the feeling obstinately persists and can stifle and overwhelm us.

How can we tackle this feeling of worthlessness, for it is not on the rational but on the emotional level? First, I think we have to recognize that we cannot get rid of it by sheer wiling. All the meditations in the world won't shake it off. Therefore it must be accepted. I have to accept its falsity and pain and then act against it—talk to God about it. When downcast at some revelation of misery, when I feel I haven't even begun in the spiritual life, when I see myself prey to evil inclinations, tempted to anger, bitterness, resentment, jealousy . . . when I am helpless, distracted at prayer, feeling completely unlovable . . . *then* is the moment for glorious confidence.

We must trust God enough to know that he would never leave us in a state of weakness without a purpose. He wants us to glorify him in it. It is at moments like these, when we feel utterly disgusted with ourselves, that we must turn to God with all our heart.

If only we had Thérèse [of Lisieux]'s insight here! She saw the grace of these bitter moments and declared them hours of joy. She prayed to God to give her an ever clearer insight into her weakness. "Where shall we find one who is truly poor in spirit?" she cries. This acceptance of self, this joyful realization of being always weak, always imperfect, is the greatest gift we can give to God. When he sees that humility is our way of being, when we have chewed on, masticated our nothingness, when we know experientially that without him we can do nothing, then he may hand us virtues—patience, fortitude, meekness, love, prayer.

It is far more important to God that we have this disposition of heart, this awareness of our nothingness, than that we should attain to sublime heights, prove to ourselves and others how holy we are, how patient, how meek, how charitable. All he asks is our goodwill. If we fail *he* is not offended, so why should *we* be upset?

The feature of God's intervention is our peaceful acceptance of our imperfection. We come to accept ourselves as we are and reality as it is. We accept our life, destiny, circumstances, other people, and we accept because we trust. God in secret is infusing knowledge of himself as love.

Finally God takes over completely. We pass from our own hands into his. Our dark, confident contemplation, has borne the fruit of union.   —*TH*, 69–71

I must say something on the Church as a whole, the Church with her self-righteous complacency, her arrogance and worldliness, who should be showing the world the face of Christ and drawing men to him; a light in the dark forest of human evil, the point of his entry into the world of men, the men he longs to give himself to. Christ suffers in his Church. In the passion at least he had his own face, but now he must hide beneath the self-satisfied, ungentle mask men hold up to it. All his beauty is effaced; his authority—"to give eternal life to all mankind"— turned into tyranny, his meekness into sentimentality, the glory of his passion disregarded under the stress of his bodily sufferings; his mother degraded to an idol, she herself unknown; his friends taken for mediators with him on our behalf as though he were not always there for us, total gift; the sacraments, his presence and saving love, looked upon as magic or automatic slot-machines.

"Sell everything and give to the poor" is his injunction to his
own, but this the Church will not do. She will not make him her
security. She must rely on her own human prudence; jealously
asserting her authority, touchy about esteem, playing safe the
whole time. Yet Peter was called to walk upon the waters. This
is what life for the Christian must be; doing what we cannot do,
with nothing to hold on to but Jesus. What a travesty that faith
means a life of peace and security! It is meant to open one to all
anguish, to walk on the edge of the world, with no security but
Jesus.

How mistaken to think that, because the Church fails to
reveal the face of her Lord, we must leave her, dishonor and
despise her. She is our mother and ever the beloved of Jesus. He
suffers her patiently and so must we. He gives himself through
her, and will always do so, and we receive him only through her.
To leave her would be to fall into the very sin we see in her, the
refusal to trust God, refusal to live without one's hands on the
controls, the whole while demanding to have things as I want
them, as seem right to me.

Jesus gives himself to men-as-they-are. This is why it should
not scandalize us that the Church is as she is and always has
been. One can say, in a sense, that it has to be like that. Jesus
put his Church into the care of Peter and at once we have him
failing in trust, succumbing to human respect and fear, betraying
the pure message with which he was entrusted.

But we cannot speak in a detached way of the Church. We
ourselves are the Church and bear responsibility for her.

—GMP, 71–72

Now it is the sad fact that many, if not most spiritual people
refuse this act of surrender. They do not accept the divine impulse
and thus never leave the ground of self. They do not give God the
opportunity of catching them up to himself; even his first, tenta-
tive approaches are rejected because they cost too much, and in
the most sensitive area of all, where I feel myself to be safe, good,
spiritually successful. The danger of this refusal is far greater

among what we might call professionals—priests, religious, and lay people who are bent on "living a spiritual life"—than among ordinary lay people who see themselves modestly trying to be good Christians, trying to please God. Only too easily we substitute the "spiritual life" or the "contemplative life" for God. Without realizing it we are intent on a self-culture. The proof is that, when God would take this out of our hands, and ask us to begin to live for him and not for our spiritual satisfaction, we refuse. God puts up with these twisted motives for as long as necessary but, if we have good will, he will try to change our direction. How passionately we cling on in the name of God. . . .

A priest might have devoted himself to work for the poor. Everyone praises him for his selfless dedication—nothing is too much trouble, nothing too irksome. Then perhaps he is asked to take charge of a well-to-do, stick-in-the-mud parish, and he objects. The reasons brought forward will be edifying because he must convince himself that he is a man of God, but the real reason is that to work in such a parish will rob him of his sense of doing something worthwhile, something heroic; it would be a spiritual come-down and would tarnish his image of himself. It may be precisely in the non-glamorous situation of an ordinary middle-class atmosphere that the greatest generosity is called for, but probably it won't feel like generosity.   —*TBJ*, 94, 96

We think of prayer as something we do for God whereas prayer is essentially a gift. Prayer is intimacy with God and it is God who offers us this intimacy. We respond. There is only one Christian prayer and that is Jesus, the New and Eternal Covenant, the union in person of God and man. All Christian prayer is essentially through him, with him, and in him. . . .

. . . The Spirit of Christ within us prompts us to pray and prays within us. What confidence this should give us, especially when our prayer seems so shoddy, hardly prayer at all. If we really believe that prayer is essentially God at work, purifying, transforming us, then we will not get discouraged when it is drab and dry.   —*LU*, 153, 155

What is this [unoccupied] prayer? I shall attempt an answer, but must grope for words. Leaving aside all other occupation and, in intention, mental preoccupation, this "me" (I shrink from saying "I" as it seems self-assertive) "looks at," "comes before," "encounters" the living God. Unoccupied prayer is equally undefended prayer. This "me" is exposed to God, stripped of pretension, naked, refusing comforting make-believe and offering itself to be gazed at, searched out and seen in total reality by the God who, in Jesus, we know to be Absolute Love. Power, holiness, justice—whatever other attributes we impute to God are nothing but expressions of God's nature as Love. It is Love that is almighty, unutterable holiness, supremely just, and so forth. "Fear not!" And this Love has the special quality of compassion, tender understanding and loving acceptance of us in all our sinfulness.

We can't disgust God. We might get fed up. God is never fed up, but always delights in us. So we can afford to be undefended and want this Love to enter every corner of our being because only then will everything in us be purified and transformed. When we pretend to ourselves and therefore to God, and when we are out to impress—ourselves first of all, but also God—with whatever holy sentiments, great desires or profound spirituality we think we have, God can't get at us! Again, we can arm ourselves with a plan of prayer we intend to carry through in order to make sure we don't get distracted for that, of course, would be to fail. What is more, we absolutely dread the awareness of how spiritually inadequate we really are and our ego takes subtle precautions to ward it off. The common dodge is to avoid altogether this undefended prayer. And this is understandable enough without faith in Jesus' God.

This God longs and longs to give, not just gifts, but himself; and it is only this supreme Gift that makes us utterly happy. We don't have to bribe him with our good works or make ourselves desirable and "worthy." His love makes us lovely. The little story of Martha and Mary expresses the truth graphically. What Jesus is saying is that, when he enters our house, that is, when we are in direct contact with him, then it is for him to give to us, to serve and feed us, not the other way round. This, I believe, represents the reality of Christian existence: receiving God, All-Love, in Christ, letting God love us, nourish us, bring us to our total fulfillment. Well nourished, we turn to our neighbors and share our nourishment with them. Freely we have received and freely we must give.

It is hard for us to hold onto this underlying truth. We turn it upside down, don't we? This is where I see the utmost importance of the prayer we are talking about: it expresses this truth as nothing else does. The Martha in us who wants to do things for God, wants to be the big one, the giver, must let go and childlike sit down with Mary at the feet of Jesus to receive. In doing so, her attitude will gradually change and her whole life, her serving, be purged of self-seeking and become in itself prayer. Our inmost heart must choose to remain a little one receiving its food from Jesus.

It is not easy to persevere faithfully in this solitary, defenseless prayer. We can be faced with seeming nothingness. What we have to realize is that the silence, the emptiness, if such be our experience, are filled with a love too great for human heart and mind to grasp. They are what seems, not what is.

Faith tells us that Love works and Its work is Love. We have but to stay there in quiet trust, even if we suffer. This is not to say that methods are barred. Yet they must be used with a light touch and not become a screen behind which we hide our spiritual impotence. Their purpose must be to help us to maintain our undefended aloneness before our God. . . .

I don't want to end by giving the impression that the sort of prayer we are discussing is necessarily bleak. At times it might be enrapturing. The point I want to emphasize is the unprotectedness, the naked exposure to "the length, the breadth, the height, the depth" of reality which is the love of God that comes to us in Christ Jesus Our Lord. We are, each one, enfolded in a love so overwhelming that it escapes conception. "As a child has rest on its mother's breast / Even so my soul" (Ps. 131:2). ". . . And he

took them in his arms, and blessed them, laying his hands upon
them" (Mark 10:16).

. . . It seems to me that this unoccupied prayer is faith at
its purest, refusing to stand on our own perception and casting
our whole weight on the Father of Jesus. Also, it is very, very
selfless: our (unfelt?) love for God overcoming self-love. Prayer
is self-surrender in faith and here, I believe, we have its purest,
personal expression.   —*LP*, 42–45

If we believe that our God is utterly self-communicating, burning with desire to love us into perfect fulfillment and happiness,
surely our fundamental attitude must be to let him do it, be
receptive and not try to control the situation ourselves.

I'm sure some techniques can be helpful to quiet us down as a
preparation for prayer, but it seems to me—I may be mistaken—
they are sometimes used as a substitute for prayer. There is the
danger of protecting ourselves from God's action by the control
we are exerting in striving to be "empty" and passive. The "I" is
very active in its attempt to surrender itself.

I am being unwise in writing on this subject as I have no
experience and can judge only by what I have read. I get the
impression of a subtle, unrecognized self-seeking, a desire to
attain a certain psychological (spiritual) experience. I find this
rather sophisticated approach to prayer hard to reconcile with
the simplicity of Jesus' words on prayer. However, God blesses
all sincere efforts and will look lovingly on all who seek him. If
we are truly seeking him, he will enlighten us. This may prove
painful. True prayer reveals us to ourselves in our sinfulness and
spiritual inadequacy and at the same time enables us to accept it
humbly and peacefully.   —*GW*, 11

While we must not go avidly seeking satisfying thoughts but
must remain quiet, exposed, surrendered, nevertheless, in one
way or another our minds must work all our life long: helpful
or tormenting, it is part of our human condition and must be
accepted wholeheartedly. Even were it to happen that we find

ourselves in a state of emotional happiness or psychic awareness—it may be emanating from a divine contact, but it need
not be so—Teresa [of Avila] counsels us still to use our minds a
little and not to allow ourselves to fall into a state of inertia and
stupidity. We can be so delighted with our feelings, so taken up
with them, that we are not taking notice of God. The fundamental act of prayer on the human side is the act of surrender, and
this always involves an act of the mind averting to his presence.
                                                              —*ICE*, 70

It is of the essence of our surrender to God that we surrender to
our neighbor too; it is largely, almost entirely in surrendering to
our neighbor that we surrender to God.   —*TBJ*, 81

If we would be utterly obedient to the "upward call" then we
must learn how to submit ourselves to others, to circumstances,
to the community welfare. Our will, our choice, must be in a
very real sense to be without choice, waiting on God, abandoned, prepared to let this or that go, to be redirected, have our
plans upset and so forth. It does not imply complete passivity,
lack of initiative; it does mean flexibility, detachment, flowing
from the faith-filled vision that discerns "it is the Lord"—the
Lord revealed not directly but through other human beings and
events.   —*AL*, 41–42

Union with Jesus consists not in sitting in glory but in sharing his cup of shame, opprobrium, dishonor, and powerlessness.
These are the things in his mind when he offers us his cup, not
the physical sufferings of his passion.
    How can we share this cup in our daily life?

> By renouncing all power and every desire for it, every
>   maneuver to obtain what we want, to prevail over
>   others;
> by taking an attitude of unimportance and subjection
>   to the community;
> by rejecting the right to insist on our rights;

> by sacrificing the image we have of ourselves and
>   which we sensitively want upheld in our own eyes
>   and that of others;
> renouncing all desire for status, of being important to
>   others.

The cup Jesus wants to share with us is that of selfless love, which is its own reward—he offers no other.

We think we know what the chalice contains and express our eagerness to drink it. When it comes to the point, when it comes to drinking the above bitter ingredients, we turn away from it with loathing.   —LL, 38

RELIGIOUS EMOTION

The following selections present Rachel's position on spiritual "experiences." What she is responding to here is "that massive weight of testimony from men and women down the centuries: that God can be experienced in some way, 'tasted,' 'seen,' 'felt'" (GMP, 45). For Rachel, there is no doubt that God's mystical presence is necessarily hidden from us: our finite humanity simply cannot lay hold of the divine life in itself. Some people may experience echoes in their psyche of God's intimate, transformative presence in their depths; however, such experiences are in no way essential to the mystical life—and are certainly not God himself. At the end of this section, we have Rachel's carefully nuanced position on what she calls the "light off" and "light on" ways of experiencing mystical union.

My conviction is that anything that can be described, given an account of, simply cannot be the mystical encounter in itself. Why is this so? Because the mystical encounter is precisely a *direct* encounter with God himself. Both Teresa [of Avila] and John [of the Cross] are quite sure of this; it is the fundamental statement they make about it: this water flows "direct from the source"; "God has drawn near," he is "very close"; and for John of the Cross it is "an inflowing of God into the soul." They see

earlier forms of prayer as "indirect"; God speaking, communicating, etc. through "natural" channels, in the "ordinary" way.
Infused or mystical contemplation is *God in direct contact*; God
himself, not a created image of him, and therefore "supernatural"
in regard to the subject; contacting in a way beyond the ordinary
faculties, therefore "supernatural" in its mode, also. This, I am
certain no one will dispute. When we insist that this encounter
with God himself, must, of its nature, bypass, or transcend our
material faculties we are saying that it must be "secret"—John
of the Cross insists on this—"from the intellect that receives it."
—*ICE*, 37–38

Now the vast majority of spiritual authors, St. Teresa [of Avila]
among them, claim that there are two paths to holiness, the
mystical way and the ordinary way. This we cannot accept. The
notion of the dual carriage-way derives from a misconception
which another modern insight has led us to correct. The mystical has been identified with certain experiences. When these are
present in a person such a one is a mystic or contemplative; he or
she has received the gift of infused contemplation, not essential
for holiness but undoubtedly a great help toward it. Inevitably
you get overtones of a high road and a low road.

   Almost at random I quote a writer typical of this view: "An
exact notion of what the mystical life really is . . . it is the sensation which the soul feels of God's presence within it, a sort of
feeling of God in the soul's centre" (cf Lejeune: *Introduction to
the Mystical Life*). He quotes a range of authors to support his
assertion—Gerson, St. Teresa, Lallement, Surin, Courbon, Pou-
lain. Firmly we deny the identification of this experience with
the mystical grace of God. This "sensation" *may* be flowing into
the psyche from God's touch on the spirit but it may equally
have another source. Not only is this "sensation" or similar
experience not the mystical grace but is not even a criterion of
its presence. Our knowledge of psychology has made us health-
ily skeptical of much of what was formerly thought to be supernatural. I want to make a careful distinction between what is

happening and what is thought to be known of this happening. "Thought to be"—the reservation is deliberate, for the mystical happening, normally, cannot be known. True there are effects, but the only reliable one is growing selflessness.

—*GMP*, 10–11

[S]anctity *is* mystical union. Surely the message of the New Testament is that union with God, divine intimacy, familiarity, unheard of privilege, is what man is for, it is the promise of the Father offered in Jesus and for which he died. We are called to be sons in the Son, heirs of God because co-heirs with Christ, sharing in the divine nature, filled with the fulness of God. If mystical union is not one and the same thing with this promise of the Father totally effected in a human being, redemption completed, then it is something bogus. There can be no higher gift than what the New Testament tells us is the common destiny of man. . . .

This Self-squanderer does not carefully weigh out his gifts, offering "divine familiarities" to a few, withholding them from others; he is not overflowing generosity to some, miserliness with others. He is always giving himself insofar as he *can* be received and he is always trying to enlarge the capacity so that he can give himself more fully. Without any doubt there are some and perhaps only the few, who have entered in this life into profoundest intimacy with God, but this intimacy, this state of mystical union simply cannot be attested by . . . psychic experiences. . . . Jesus himself gives us the criterion. It is loving "as I have loved you," keeping his commandments as he keeps his Father's, it is living as he did in total surrender. This conformity with Jesus, this total surrender, is impossible to human effort, a divine gift is needed, an infusion of divine energy, the Spirit of Jesus himself, the Promise of the Father. This is precisely what we mean by mystical, infused contemplation.   —*ICE*, 41–42

When I have been writing about prayer, I have made a point of addressing myself to those who experience little or no religious emotion in order to encourage them. I do this because it would seem that spiritual writers tend to take it for granted that, sooner or later, consolation will come, and that we must indeed persevere in difficulties which are sure to be there, but looking forward to the day when the sun will shine. Almost always the implication, even though very subtle, is that consolation is the real thing, real prayer. The writer might deny this and yet, it seems to me, that as often as not the implication is there. This, I believe, has to be firmly refuted. In no way is it decrying the reality of consolation and its desirability, but it may not be iden-tified with prayer itself. It may accompany prayer, but prayer is equally real without it.   —*LP*, 74

I want to make a distinction between two ways of experienc-ing mystical union. By this I do not merely refer to full and transforming union, the culmination of the spiritual life, but to those partial unions which happen all along the way, when God touches our being with his own and for that instant unites it to himself. This includes those first early touches when being itself is so dwarf-like that the union is minimal. . . . [I]n all mystical union from first to last there are two different ways of experi-ence, that I call "light off" and "light on."

To say that, when God touches being with his own being, when he would give himself to us as God, he must necessar-ily by-pass the ordinary routes into the self and create one for himself which only he can use, is at the same time saying that this visitation, this contact is, of itself, inaccessible to ordinary perception. By the very nature of things it must be secret, hid-den. This normal, proper obscurity I call "light off." Something unspeakably wonderful is happening in the depths of self and the self cannot see it. No light shines on it. There are effects flow-ing from this happening and these are consciously experienced, but not the happening itself. "Light off" is the normal mode.

However, it is possible for God to switch on a light, so to speak, then what is happening is "seen." What this faculty is by which we "see," I do not know. What I want to stress is that

the fundamental happening is the same; the switching on of the
light does not add to it or change it in any way. For this to be
the usual mode of receiving the mystical embrace is exceedingly
rare, and this is another point I wish to stress, for I fear it has
not been appreciated. A "light on" state as distinct from an occa-
sional reception of "light on" may perhaps occur no more than
once or twice in an era. It has a prophetic character. The one so
endowed understands beyond the ken of human kind and he or
she must enlighten others. This light throws its beams on the
ordinary way and enables us to understand it. . . .

. . . [A]s it is a question of God himself, this seeing is non-conceptual; it simply cannot be held by the mind, looked at, still less
described. . . .

It must be stressed that for neither "light on" or "light off"
have we claimed any distinguishing "favors." This is crucial.
What a world of misunderstanding here! It would be a complete
misconception to think of "light on" as a state abounding in
"favors" such as St. Teresa [of Avila] describes: her prayer of
quiet, union, rapture, ecstasy. The essential experience of "light
on" is non-conceptual, it cannot be handled by the mind. It is
indistinct and all-pervading. It has nothing to do with "things
happening."

But say a "light on" person wanted to describe as best he
could what he saw of God holding the soul, even the first light
holding we described, which the soul ordinarily experiences as
aridity, then, profoundly moved by what he saw, he might pour
out the most extravagant images, all the while knowing that his
words were totally inadequate to give any idea of this ineffable,
non-conceptual reality.   —*GMP*, 45–46, 47, 49

What must it be to "see" God loving us? Is it any wonder that
Teresa [of Avila] was ravished with joy? It does us good to read
her outpourings, even to read of her psychic response provided
we understand it, for it is not easy in our everyday lives, in
our greyness and dryness, to keep our hearts aloft, to keep the
mountain top before our eyes. We can go for encouragement

and refreshment to the one who "saw." True, her own mode of expression, her choice of imagery may not appeal to us but at least we perceive the rapture of one who "saw" in a similar way in which the apostles "saw" the risen Lord. We can be inspired and encouraged without in any way desiring a like vision for "blessed are they who have not seen and yet believe." We must be absolutely convinced . . . that exactly the same grace of intimacy is offered to us; we too can be totally transformed in love even in this life. "Sight" such as Teresa had is given only to the few but when as in her case, she shares something of her sense of blinding Reality, we can happily accept the stimulation to our own faith and desire.   —*ICE*, 78

THESE WONDERFUL, MYSTICAL GIFTS

In this final set of selections, Rachel relates her insight that the sacraments not only nurture us on our spiritual journey but are, in fact, concentrated expressions of the essence of the mystical life. In their various ways, the sacraments are embodiments of our call to be taken by the Spirit into Jesus's self-emptying surrender to the Father's total self-gift of love.

Catholicism is profoundly sacramental. In this way it, constantly, practically affirms that everything is given to us; our sanctification is a divine—not a human—work; we cannot make our own way to God but God has come to us in Jesus who himself has become our worship, our perfect offering, our union with the Father, our life, our holiness, our atonement.

A careful study of the liturgy of the sacraments will deepen our insight and we shall avoid the danger of seeing the sacraments as no more than sacred rites, duties we have to perform, in order to please God. Sadly, these wonderful, mystical gifts can fall into the category of meritorious works, a keeping of the law that gives us a claim on God. They are living, loving encounters, each one of them, with our Savior, Jesus, who himself is one with God. Jesus is the important one. He is the giver the doer, the offererer, the beloved of God. We come to the sacraments to be taken up in him. "This is my body given for you. What I have done for you, you must do for others." You too must be "for others." We come from the liturgy of the Mass and the other sacraments into the equally sacred liturgy of our daily lives. The sacramental character of the Church is a clear sign that there is no distinction between the sacred and the profane and that the whole of creation is holy and open to God.   —*LM*, 89–90

The sacraments are direct encounters with God in Christ. In them God touches us directly, he himself, unmediated. This is the mystical life in concentrated form, flashing out in all its intolerable brightness for one vitalizing minute. But we can only take this brightness in the measure we are there for it. Conversely, the more we expose what we are, however small that may be, the more there becomes of us. It can only be in utter mystery. What happens at communion? Confession? No human mind can comprehend the encounter because it is of its essence too personally God.   —*GMP*, 29

Popularly it is taken for granted that those of us who are baptized Christians, who try to serve God following our Lord, are already in the kingdom, we belong to those blessed ones who "receive him" and are therefore made his children born not of flesh, not of the will of man but of God. In other words, we have received our new birth, our whole being is now supernatural and so is our prayer. Too easily, promise, potentiality have been expressed in terms of facts, fulfillment. If we look carefully at the gospels have we any reason for thinking that we, unlike others, have received the kingdom? Are we shown anyone in the gospels who actually did? Are we better than they? The point is that Jesus was rejected, even by his own. When the hour of scandal came they lost faith. Our baptism, the privilege of our Christian calling is affirming that *this* mystical union is what life is for, this is what God is calling us to do, this is our vocation. It is not a "hey presto," it is done.   —*ICE*, 54

Jesus has left with us a sacred rite whereby his perfect surrender to his Father, enacted all his life long, reaching its climax in his death, is concretized at a specific moment here for us; for us, precisely, so that we can deliberately, with most full intent make it our own. In the Mass we have the deepest expression of what prayer is. Here God does everything. Here Jesus, his beloved, offers himself, the perfect offering of perfect love in which his Father delights. He delights in it because it gives him the supreme, eagerly desired opportunity to lavish himself on man. The reward of Jesus' surrender—and in what untold pain and darkness it was made and with what untold confidence and love—was God himself. Daily we have in our hands this perfect prayer as our very own.

We must make it more and more our own, and this means surrendering ourselves with his surrender so that we too might receive the Father's love to his heart's content. Again, this is not a part-time thing. Jesus' surrender to his Father was not a part-time thing, it was his very way of being, and so must it be with us. At Mass, we renew over and over again our will to surrender with Jesus; from this sacrament flows the power of God to enable us to do so. It is the sacrament of union; every participation in it deepens our union with our Lord, a union which we must then live out in our everyday life. It is our very offerings, our bread and wine, fruits of our earth and works of our hands, that are transformed into the sacrifice of Jesus. What clearer message of the meaning of our work-a-day life? . . .

Our reception of Holy Communion is saying "Amen" to what Jesus is doing and "Amen" to his summons to us to enter into his saving death. He will give us understanding of this death, showing us how it is to be fulfilled in our daily life. Only he can show us.

Much the same can be said of the sacrament of reconciliation or confession. Here the encounter with the savior is focused on forgiveness of sin, the recognition and public acknowledgment that we have sinned and that only in Jesus can we be reconciled with the Father and with our brethren. It is not merely the opportunity for us to express frequently, verbally, our sorrow for our lack of love, our selfishness and carelessness, but actually to receive our Lord's own sorrow for sin and his perfect atonement. Only he can really understand how closed and unloving we are; only he can do something about it. This sacrament makes plain to us that our own trifling sorrow and efforts at atonement get us nowhere; they are of value only when caught up in the column of loving worship rising on earth from the heart of Jesus.

Is there anything less satisfying on the human level than frequent confession? It demands perhaps a greater effort of faith than does the Mass. The presence and action of Jesus is most deeply hidden. We feel that we can never do justice in words to whatever we ourselves understand of our shoddiness, still less to what it is in reality. But of course we don't have to. God sees our heart. All that matters is faith in Jesus, a coming to him for his knowledge, his sorrow, his atonement. We are happy then at the poverty of our own sentiments. We can be sure that when we come time and time again to this sacrament, with what we see and what we don't see of our selfishness, our Lord is able to work in us, purifying and healing us, every bit as powerfully as when he bade the palsied man arise and summoned Lazarus from the tomb.

Sorrow for sin is not an emotion and need not, though it may be, accompanied by emotion. It consists in a determination to do what we can to change, and surely one of its chief manifestations will be the desire to approach the sacrament given us for the purpose.   —*TBJ*, 80, 82–83

6

Transformed into the Gift of God

*If the kingdom does impregnate the world of men it can
only be because individual hearts have received it. Only
individuals, transformed into love are the presence of
Love in the world.*

—ICE, 43

*In this chapter we contemplate with Rachel the mystery of being
transformed into the gift of God. What does it mean to be so
receptive to God's outpoured love that we ourselves become the
presence of Love in the world? What does it mean to have so
allowed the crucified Jesus to unite the poverty of our being with
his "Yes" to the Father's love that it is no longer we who live, but
Jesus who lives in us? This is the culmination of the mystical life,
the third stage of the spiritual journey.*

*If Rachel has been robust and comprehensive in her presen-
tations of the previous two stages, here she tends toward reti-
cence. Throughout her writings, this stage is the least discussed.
Accounting for this, Rachel comments, "It is only in the first
stages that we really need guidance. Once we have been drawn
into the luminous darkness which is Jesus, he is our light" (TBJ,
viii).*

*Moreover, the summit of the spiritual life is ultimately inef-
fable. While something needs to be said about this wonder of
becoming Jesus, this being taken completely into the divine*

communion of love, we are in a realm where human words quickly fall short.

A LIFE OF LOVE

The passages in this section explore the essence of transformation into the gift of God. What emerges is a condition of glorious paradoxes. As we consent for the full scope of our human vulnerability and powerlessness to be taken into Jesus's surrendered heart, we become both wholly alive with the divine life and most fully ourselves.

A full flowering of the mystical life and the Christian life are one and the same thing. The culmination, perfection, fulfillment of the Christian life—"all that the Lord has promised"—is, in our special terminology, the mystical marriage or transforming union. The ascent of Mount Carmel is but the fulness of the Christian life, which is synonymous with the fulness of human being. There are not two vocations, one to human fulfillment and the other, if we are special and privileged, to Christian fulfillment. There is only *one* fulfillment to be achieved either in this world or the next, that which we call mystical marriage or transforming union.   —*AL*, 1

To be holy means that a human being has so affirmed, stood by, embraced her essential meaning of being a capacity for God, an emptiness for God to fill, that God has filled her with the fullness of himself.   —*QUD*, 33

We must therefore look for what is the essence of union, or rather the essential "quality" of the person in the state of union. What *must* be true of her no matter what her psychological repercussions? Total receptivity means total selflessness and this means that God is truly all in this heart. There is no ego on the summit of the mountain, only the honor and glory of God. This must be understood literally. John [of the Cross] has labored to

show us how to surrender the whole of ourselves to the Lord,
all the powers of soul and body, memory, understanding, and
will, interior and exterior senses, the desires of spirit and sense.
This is done progressively both as a generous and unremitting
effort on our part and by the divine enablement and purgation.
Now it is truly accomplished; it has happened. The bride has no
desires of the will, no acts of understanding, neither object nor
occupation of any kind which she does not refer wholly to God,
together with all her desires. We may want this to happen, we
may, and indeed must, aim at it; but rarely, says John, is it an
actual fact; rarely is a life totally God's. The true bride however
is "taken up" with God, absorbed with him. She is all love. All
her activities are love, all her strength and energies are concentrated in love. Love is most truly her sole occupation whatever
else she is doing. Like the wise merchant in our Lord's parable
she has gladly squandered everything for the supreme treasure,
the whole purpose and fulfillment of human being in which lies
the honor and glory of God. She is never after her own will, her
own gratification, nor is she merely following her own inclinations. She is never engaged in anything that is in the slightest
degree alien to him. Her mind is occupied in considering what
he wants of her, what will most serve him; her will is in desiring
him alone: "My sole occupation is love." Here is complete loss
of self-love (which we have termed the ego), here is a transcendence that has reached its term, is joined now for ever to what
it belongs to. . . .

. . . Hers is inviolable strength, not as from herself, for she
remains poor and weak as well she knows, but from the God
who possesses her and communicates to her his own strength.
She lives by his life, his virtue, his wisdom, his love; hence her
utter security. The bride can never be wrested from this absolute
safety. She has chosen to abandon all for his sake, to lose her
very self and live in deep solitude. So now God assumes full care
of her, holds her in his arms, feeds her with all good things and
takes her into his deepest secrets. He is now her sole guide and

works in her directly and immediately all the time. She is entirely under the influence of the Holy Spirit, moved by him and him alone. . . .

Does not the figure of Jesus inevitably rise before the eyes of our mind? Have we not described precisely what the gospels reveal of Jesus, the Father's beloved? John of the Cross speaks of the deification of the human person, becoming God, being equal as it were to God. How this can be misinterpreted unless we keep our eyes on Jesus. John has bidden us do this throughout. Jesus is a receptivity so absolute that he is true God of true God; the Father is able to communicate himself to him in fulness. In his humble mortal life, a life like ours, of hours and days, he sees the Father always and everywhere and lives out of that vision. Thus it is that "he who sees me sees the Father." It is the Father who speaks through him, who acts through his total obedience and receptivity, because he *can* speak and act through him. Jesus is truly human because he is divine. He lives God-life humanly. He is God's human existence.

Human being only becomes what it is when it is handed over, given up and lost in the incomprehensible mystery of God. In Jesus this open-ended, self-abandoning, self-transcendent being has attained its goal, that toward which by its very essence it strives, and it is to him we come with our own empty infinitude for completion in him. We do not expect our life's experience to be different from his. He was as totally possessed by his Father in his earthly life when he worked and ate and slept, when he wept with pain and frustration, when he felt abandoned and desolate on the cross, as he now is in glory. The servant is not above his master. As the Father communicates himself fully to Jesus, so Jesus communicates himself fully to his bride—all that the Father has given me—ALL, literally. The bride therefore shares most profoundly in Jesus' salvific work of bringing everyone to the Father. "One single act of pure love is of greater potency than all other works put together," and here is, not one single act, but a life of love.   —*AL*, 115, 116–17

Friends of God? Can it be? Yes, but there is only one way: to become "son"; to accept the friendship and companionship of Jesus so as to learn sonship from him, share in his sonship. In practice this means being utterly unimportant to ourselves, becoming selfless, empty, nothing but an echo—like Enoch disappearing. This is the paradox: the one who has consented to be nothing but an emptiness for the Father's love, becomes—and only now, in this context of nothingness, dare we breathe the word—somehow "equal" to God, raised up to be his friend, his beloved. "The Father and I are one," says Jesus. Lost in his *kenosis* it can perhaps be said of us.   —*OF*, 22

> I made a garden for God.
> No, do not misunderstand me
> It was not on some lovely estate or even in a pretty
>   suburb.
> I made a garden for God
> in the slum of my heart:
> a sunless space between grimy walls
> the reek of cabbage water in the air
> refuse strewn on the cracked asphalt—
> the ground of my garden!
> This was where I labored
> night and day
> over the long years
> in dismal smog and cold—
> there was nothing to show for my toil.
> Like a child I could have pretended:
> my slum transformed . . .
> an oasis of flowers and graceful trees
> how pleasant to work in such a garden!
> I could have lost heart
> and neglected my garden
> to do something else for God.
> But I was making a garden for God
> not for myself

for his delight not mine
and so I worked on in the slum of my heart.
Was he concerned with my garden?
Did he see my labor and tears?
I never saw him looking
never felt him there
Yet I knew (though it felt as if I did not know)
that he was there with me
waiting . . .
He has come into his garden
Is it beautiful at last?
Are there flowers and perfumes?
I do not know
the garden is not mine but his —
God asked only for my little space
to be prepared and given.
This is "garden" for him
and my joy is full.

TBJ, 101–2

Up to the present the person has given what she possessed, all the substance of her house, and only implicitly gave herself, but now it is specifically herself that is given or rather taken. Who can grasp what this means, the extent of this gift? It is death, but a death that is life, true life. The person is taken away from herself and that permanently. What will it be to live without a "self," to exist as a wraithlike thing? Looked at from the purely human angle, terrible indeed, but not when it is the effect of God becoming all in all. This is perfect human fulfillment and heaven on earth.

Hitherto, God's union with us was temporary and partial, now it is permanent, total. Only now can we really speak of an indwelling. In essence it is a state of rapture, that is, the self taken out of the self and that abidingly. There is no counterpart in nature. It can be understood only in the incarnation. It derives from this and, as someone dared to suggest, can be called an extension of it. A person in this state is totally possessed by Jesus, identified with him in his surrender to his Father. Thus, through her, Jesus is on earth in an incomparable way. His kingdom has come in her and because of this comes even more fully into the world.

Up to now we have spoken of the person knowing, loving, surrendering; we can do so no longer, for being is identified with its activities: she *is* love, *is* surrender. In this sense we can say that faith is transcended. The mysteries of faith, which on the second island were entered into and became principles of living, are now simply Jesus. This happy creature is at last fully Christian, fully human. —*GMP*, 117–18

Jesus expressly declares that he has nothing of himself: the works he does are not his but his Father's; the judgments he makes are dictated by the Father; the whole initiative of his life derives from the Father. He exists as a sort of emptiness through which the Father speaks and acts. At the same time, paradoxically, he exists as a highly individual man firm in decision, act, and judgment. There is nothing cipher-like in his personality. This is the mystery: man is that being who only becomes himself when he has surrendered totally to God; only when he is lost to himself is he fully *there*. Jesus experienced himself as having no life of his own, no power, no wisdom. All these he derived from his Father. On our side, we derive all from Jesus. As the Father is his life, so Jesus is ours and thus the Father is ours. One with Jesus we live with him in the Father, from the Father. We must not think for a moment that transformation into Jesus robs a person of individuality, that from henceforth they have no emotions, no preferences, no interests. Transformation into Jesus means we become fully human. —*ICE*, 115

Those in the third island are identified with Jesus. He surrenders to the Father in them and each of their lives is sealed with his. As John of the Cross says, they enter deeper and deeper into the caverns of Christ, into an understanding of his incarnation, death, and resurrection—not a notional understanding but an immersion in these very mysteries. Now the sacraments come into their own. That which formerly could be received only partially, now meets with no obstacle. The unutterably "alien" and "other," God himself, meets in the soul a life "other" to its depths. The sacramental encounter is continuous. Two abysses meet and know one another. Every reception of the sacraments means a deeper surrender and possession by God and always it is in the Church and for the Church.   —*GMP*, 132

It is generally accepted that those in the state of transforming union are confirmed in grace, that they cannot sin. This is simply explained. Looked at from their angle: throughout the long arduous journey across the second island they were unremittingly choosing God, saying "yes" to every demand. Their whole being has, so to speak, set in that direction and cannot change; theoretically they can change but in fact they cannot. . . . But there is the other side, God's. It has been mutual giving; continually he has drawn a person into himself and this embrace has evoked greater surrender. The time comes when he can take her completely, hold her so deeply and constantly within himself that she can go out no more. How could she sin? God cannot fail himself. If by an impossibility she could break out of this blessed prison, then of course she would sin, but she cannot; her own structure, built of endless surrenders, and in God's safe keeping makes this impossible. This is another blessedness of this state, the certainty that one can never go back, that one is safe for ever; in a very real sense the goal is reached.

This does not mean such a person cannot grow or enter more deeply into God. There is still work to be done, but it is not a question of striving, for struggle is over, but rather deeper and deeper surrender, letting God do everything, and totally sure that he will do so. Again there is the blessedness of certitude. She cannot displease God, she is always his delight but she can please him less, so to speak, and this she must watch. It is probable that she could court death and God would grant her desire, because he will do all she wills, and she cannot will contrary to his will. All the same it could mean more to him to have her stay on earth, grow still more and give him greater love, it would seem probable that he would want her to remain on earth some time, perhaps many years. Nor is she perfect. The roots of sin are cut, but maybe some droopy little bits of green are still there—feelings of jealousy, annoyance, contrariness, but they are absolutely harmless, mere feelings, rather like those that remain when a limb has been amputated. She does not ask for them to go, because she knows they do not matter. Yes, she is not afraid to compare them with the wounds of Jesus, which still remain, tokens of a bloody struggle but a struggle that is over. She does not have to struggle against these feelings, they are there to keep her holding out her hand to Jesus.

I think this lowly note is the right one on which to stop discussion of a transformed being, affirming a holiness that is pure gift flowing over from him who alone is holy. Jesus is her holiness, and her holiness is human and not faultless. It is a holiness that accepts what man really is and what he must suffer, a holiness which is of non-alluring arduousness; Jesus made it clear to us. But we want a "splendid way," a "quick way," a "way to keep our dignity and enhance it" while Jesus lived out a life of fundamental "ordinariness."   —*GMP*, 146–48

LETTING GOD BE GOD IN US

In the following selections, Rachel grapples with the lived experience of life that is both fully human and fully divine. We see that the very nature of this state makes it impossible to speak about the lived experience of it in generalized terms: if we become our fully realized selves at the summit, then our experience of it is uniquely our own. The great treasure of this section is the glimpse we are given of Rachel's particular experience; she uses the guise of "Petra," and her experience is related to us partly through an exchange of letters between Petra and her friend "Claire." While Petra's lived experience of the summit bears little resemblance to

that of St. Teresa of Avila or St. John of the Cross, they all share
essentially the same state.

A characteristic of the state of spiritual marriage is that it is different, absolutely, from all that has gone before it. It is incommunicable and remains the individual's lived experience for which
there are no words, no ideas. Let an attempt be made to describe
it and inevitably it is put within the range of the familiar. A
gulf lies between the spiritual marriage and anything that can
be remotely touched upon in word and image. One mystic may
express his or her experience as anguish, another as joy.

—*AL*, 5

To avoid any notion of pantheism or loss of identity, we must
return to the principle that the individuality, the distinction, the
otherness of the creature is established in direct proportion to its
nearness to the creator. The more surrendered to and possessed
by God, the more immersed in God, the more the self is self.
This individualization at its highest peak means that there is no
pattern of living on the third island. On the former islands there
were patterns; to some extent one could generalize, but here
hardly at all. Each inhabitant of this island is a world, a universe
of her own. We can only listen to what each tries to tell us of her
experience and see where other testimony agrees.   —*GMP*, 119

Although theoretically we know better, most of us find it difficult
to see the true face of holiness. Instinctively we remove it from
all that is too natural or "worldly," as we would say. Of course
we accept that a saint is human but, on the whole, we find it
impossible to take on the full implications of this. We would not
readily acclaim as holy one who was a shrewd businesswoman
who took over the management of her brother's financial affairs
because she knew more about such things than he did; or a
woman who was well aware of her captivating charm and never
thought of dimming the headlights but allowed them full play,
to the delight of all who approached her—more than that, who

consciously employed this charm to gain her own ends. Nor do we readily associate with sanctity one who admitted unashamedly to feeling hurt when her love was not returned, annoyed and angry at times. But it is here that we come up against something crucial to holiness that is little appreciated. Teresa [of Avila]'s will was identified with that of our Lord and so everything she was, both her many gifts and her weaknesses, were brought into the orbit of her love and dedication. Union with Christ does not mean becoming someone different, renouncing our gifts, changing our temperament, but putting everything we have into our love for God and opening everything we are to his transforming influence. Teresa's business acumen, her charm, her wit: everything was caught up into her self-offering to him. And it is above all in her letters that her richly various personality is revealed; there, too, her sanctity.

For this woman, God, revealed to her in Jesus, is the sole Reality. She lived always face to face with Reality. All else— people, events, commonplace things such as medicines, cooking stoves, lawsuits, illnesses, a lizard in a cornfield, a beautiful morning in May when the birds are singing, the cold, rain, floods (cause of so much suffering), the discomfort of the springless wagons in which she journeyed, the bad inns—all the multitudinous events of her life were real to her, had meaning for her only in God. Teresa reached the full potential of personhood; what she was meant to be, she became. This is holiness. Whatever our stature, great or little; whatever our talents, many or few; everything must be given over to God, unified, directed by the desire to make God our all. Teresa was not afraid of humanness. No gift that God, through circumstances, asked her to develop was left to wither. Develop it she did, unafraid, looking only to him, his approval, not wondering whether she was conforming to an image of holiness or not. That quiet bleeding to death of cancer of the womb has its own poignancy. The medical cause of her death was concealed from her nuns, presumably because it seemed too unworthy of a saint: too natural, earthy, sexual.

—*EP*, 92–93

Do many attain holiness in this life? We have Jesus' answer that few find the straight road to life; and holiness is life, eternal life with the Father here in this world. To be virtuous, very virtuous does not, of itself, mean holiness. The human ego, coveting its own security and glory, can build a magnificent palace of virtue. A holy person will also be virtuous, but it will be in the way our Lord was. Those who secretly seek their own glory will follow a pattern of virtuous living, an accepted pattern and be deeply concerned not to depart from it. Hence their narrow-mindedness, their lack of flexibility and freedom. The holy person will not be concerned with patterns, but every moment will be looking to our Lord to learn how to live. They may well depart from the accepted pattern and thus others may fail to recognize their holiness. It seems to me that this will usually be the case, as with St. Thomas More, St. Thérèse [of Lisieux] and St. Bernadette. But as Jesus' friend cares nothing for himself this does not weigh with him at all. He isn't interested.   —*TBJ*, 103

We are trying now to answer the question: "What does someone know of this world-shattering experience? How does she know?" All of us can read what Teresa [of Avila] and John [of the Cross] have to say and somehow, vaguely, just because they are "light on" we recognize that of course they would know, for they would "see," "see" God in possession. Teresa expresses it in terms of a vision of the Trinity dwelling within her, and similarly John. As Claire belongs to this category, I asked her if she could say anything about her experience, how she knew she had passed into the state of transforming union. With great reserve she replied: "Jesus has always been my music, but the music was all I noticed. I wasn't aware, before, that it was in some way 'I' who played, or 'I' who was the organ. But after he brought me to the third island, I found the difference. He was now all. The music played of itself—there was *only* the music. I was now living what had seemed my life before, but only seemed because I only looked at him and didn't advert to myself. Now myself has become him." . . .

It will be useful here to look at Petra. I quote from a letter to Claire:

It was my "hermit day" and I had an extraordinary sense of peace, as though nothing could ever touch me again. This peace had been growing for some weeks but, being occupied with the community and other things, I hadn't stopped to taste it. This day, completely free from everything, it flooded into my consciousness and wrapped me round. I was in the garden, and for a moment I seemed to be looking within and I saw or realized in a mysterious way that *I* was not there. There was no "I." I can't say more than that. *I* had gone. It wasn't that I saw or felt God, but it was as if I were in a vast and lonely plain far removed from everything. For a few weeks I lived to some extent outside myself, by which I mean only a very small part of me seemed in contact with what was going on around me. I had similar experiences of this estrangement in earlier days but they were extremely bitter. This was bewildering joy. I felt physically and nervously exhausted but I managed to carry on, and I do not think anyone saw anything was different with me. I longed to tell you and then I decided against it. If what I believed was really true, then with your usual insight you would know it without my saying it and this would be a confirmation. So when we met I said nothing. We were discussing the mansions and the state of union. I said as casually as I could that I thought de Caussade had something to say when he spoke of the soul living in God and God living in the soul. There was silence. You felt ill and suggested we walked in the fresh air. Still you made no comment. But next day you wrote to me telling me that, when I said those words you saw what had happened and were overwhelmed. This confirmation was precious to me. "You have given me more joy than I ever expected would be mine, because I see you wholly his."

Well, this state of bewildered happiness lasted a couple of weeks, and then I found myself in the wasteland. But the sense of estrangement continued to some extent and is with me still. I know that, in reality, I have died
. . .

Later bewildered in her new state, she wrote of her pain to Claire, who replied:

This is really what joy means, isn't it? Nothing but God—and God apparently not there . . . so that the whole soul is gift, is surrender, is that "lived nothingness" we spoke of. When I said that you were conscious of yourself, this is what I meant: that your experience is of *what you are*, that is, an emptiness God has filled. But you are never shown the fulness, God, the sole reason for your being emptied—all you see is the creature side. You call it "blind will that clings, or rather, is held." If you could see the holding, you would forget all the anguish of being that blind, subhuman thing—all would vanish in the light of the Holy One to whom the will is soldered. I don't think, given this experiential darkness, which is mystical light and hence unseen, that you would ever be able, in full confidence, to believe in his having taken possession. That was why I once suggested you should write it down. I knew the days were coming when the sheer weight of darkness would make what your heart told you a mockery. But you know it is not. You know at a depth deeper than any darkness, a depth the "darkness cannot overcome" that God has made you his. Are *you* paying the price? Is it not Jesus, as you gropingly wonder? To know the full smallness, the incompleteness of being human, to open wholly to the suffering and frustration and endless pettiness of living: it is Jesus who knows that, who is living it in you and living it in radiant happiness. Secretly you know this, you know the weariness and pain is the shadow that tells you he is there. His sacramental signs . . .

Petra had some sort of initial "light on" experience. Was it a "light on"? I asked her about it. She said that, compared with all that has followed it was "light on," but of a negative nature, if that is not a contradiction. Her point seems to be that it was not God she saw, she saw emptiness, saw that self had gone. That experience has never been recaptured in so vivid a way. This seems a far cry from Teresa's vision of the glorious Christ celebrating his nuptials with her and yet have we any reason to doubt that it is fundamentally the same grace? Basically it is the fulfillment of our Lord's words, "If anyone loves me he will keep my word and my Father will love him, and we will come to him and make our abode with him." Those for whom the light is on, as with Claire and St. Teresa, have a glimpse of this hidden reality. The basic difference is that the one sees it from God's side, sees God at work, the other sees it from the human, sees the consequent emptiness. . . .

The experience of lowliness and emptiness consequent on this sublime state must be emphasized. Let us listen to Petra again:

Your letter, with its comfort, was very timely. My long silence has been due in great part to lack of time, suffi-cient, uninterrupted, relaxed time for writing a deeply personal letter, but partly because I have been so bruised and weary that, when I sat down to write, my spirit failed me. Your letter, with its uncanny insight, seemed to break down whatever was making me inarticulate. No, it is not doubt that plagues me; your letter only confirms what my heart knows but it means so much, in bewildering obscurity, to have another's voice affirm-ing. No, no, I never expected that there is a short-cut that by-passes the drudgery of human experience. I don't want one, I want to drink to the dregs the chal-ice of my Lord. In my case (and isn't this the common, ordinary state?) how non-glamorous, ignoble this chalice! What does it amount to with me? A sense of inner fragility and faintness, which taps, knocks at the wall of my body too. I seem unable to face up to any pressure. I feel faced with an immense "trial" utterly beyond myself, and yet when I look, where is the trial? What have I to suffer compared with so many people? I have good health, am surrounded with love, have everything I need, and yet life itself seems more than I can bear—the unutterable loneliness and emptiness, the mystery and obscurity. Yesterday, I heard of a poor woman enduring humiliating helplessness for ten years, and now, faced with new symptoms, her splendid spirit is breaking and she can take no more. Just one of millions similarly suffering from seemingly unbearable afflictions. And what relation has my life to hers? By comparison I have nothing to suffer. It is my hope that this "suffering" of mine which is nameless, which really has no right to be called suffering, this inner "dissolution" should be a way through which Jesus comes to others in their grief and pain. I feel overwhelmed with everything: with the beauty of the world, with its terrible pain, with its evil and ugliness, the devilish brutality of man to man—with the Word of God so mighty and so obscure. I could weep my eyes out with—I don't know what! Oh, how fragile I am, without achievement; no human victory, no human beauty, only that which is he, who experienced in all its raw bitterness the human condition.

Occasionally I am overwhelmed by emotional turmoil, tumultuous feelings of disgust and revolt. I seem swept off my feet by what I cannot control. It could be frightening, indeed it is frightening, and yet sheer experience shows me that I am safe, that the crashing waves of temptation break harmlessly against the walls of my citadel. "Crashing waves of temptation," what grandiose words for the petty things I mean: an arrangement that upsets me, the feeling of being a powerless member of a group, without rights of privacy, the pressure of community life on a very independent woman, who is not by nature a community woman—all the nothings that go to make the grinding routine of religious life or any life. Of course, my temperament has a lot to do with this, others wouldn't react so strongly or be in such a degree conscious of the "tears of things." But my heart tells me the Lord is in it; this lowly way is his way. In the sight of men I seem to fail—but in God's eyes? I ask to tread no other path. I am content to feel these difficulties to the end of my life. He has taught me, and still teaches me the human can't which becomes his glorious fiat. . . .

"Unimportance," yes, Claire, I feel that is the best word to express a vital point. "Littleness," "helplessness," "poverty" can be run to death and lose their life. "Non-importance" carries with it a dreadful awareness of one's basic insecurity and meaninglessness. It's not only a question of being non-important in one's community, business and so on, it is on the cosmic level also. Isn't this one of the frightening experiences of us moderns—the unimportance, the vulnerability and fragility of man? It might seem that we Christians who are striving to live out what we believe, who see our meaning in God, who know, in faith, the grandeur and security of man in God, can let go this craving for importance. Oh, but we can't. We carry on the pursuit in a far more subtle and dangerous way. We want spiritual importance. We want our interior life, our way to God, to have elements which make us feel important. We want to rise above the mediocrity of the common lot. This might seem justifiable but in reality it could mean nothing but a desire for a more interesting form of spiritual life, a desire to escape from the sheer drabness of the ordinary, seeking a short-cut from the drudgery . . . back again to that secret coveting of spiritual riches, beauty, glory, achievement.

To be unimportant as a child—seemingly so simple, it is the hardest thing a human being can do, to accept that it depends utterly on God, to let go its petty, sham securities, to abandon itself unreservedly in darkness and pain, in light and joy, it matters not, to God. For this, Jesus lived and died, and this is the substance of his work in us in all that befalls.

How different this lowly admission from the ideas usually formed of the state of transforming union and which mystical writers seem to affirm. . . .

Your vocation to poverty (writes Claire to Petra) fills me with holy awe . . . how utterly destructive it is of what human pride regards as self-evident if it is to be a saint. It is all very well to speak of "self-dissatisfaction" but oh, in practice, what it means of trust in God and an acceptance of the truth. No comforting evasions here—not even the happy glow of knowing one is all one would wish—not even wishing really, except for him to have the pleasure. It is impossible to live this utter destitution except in Jesus . . . your very state of accepted "nothingness" is the radiant proof that you are his. It is mystical in the strictest sense. No one would even *know* it pleased God unless Jesus revealed it from within.

Petra has a profound grasp that her stark, human experience is mystical, that it is, in fact, Jesus living it in her. "Son of God though he was, he learned obedience through what he suffered." Was not this school of suffering precisely the experience of what it means to be a man and to die, to be born dying? No one has ever plumbed the depths of human littleness and wretchedness as he did; no one ever tasted the bitter draught of human poverty as he. His very sinlessness heightened the awareness of this poverty. Yet Jesus never evaded it, he lived it out fully to the inevitable end, death. . . .

. . . Ingrained in us is this longing for a beautiful spiritual life, to be beautiful for God! Jesus shows us what is beautiful in God's eyes: the total acceptance of lowliness and the surrender of that lowliness to the Father's love. Jesus, by living it through to the end, carried it all to the Father. He delivered the pitiable human condition from meaninglessness, drew the fangs of suffering and death. All is changed now. Nothing is just what it seems to be. Outwardly it seems the same but it is a different reality. This is what it means to live the risen life of Jesus. It does not mean living in a euphoric or exalted state. Essentially it means letting God be God in us. Oh, how little is this understood even by those who think they understand it. . . .

Petra is aware, more at some times than at others, that all save a tiny portion of her is absorbed elsewhere. She is not aware of what she is absorbed in, what she is knowing or loving, she just knows that she is in some way being devoured. She cannot get at this inner reality and never tries to. She is content just to be; life passes by, passes over her; she feels, reacts, can be hurt, cast down, groan under the pressure of life, and in another sense be "away," almost with a sense of non-being which can frighten at times. Below the level of superficial doubts and questionings is an assurance, an inability to worry or be anxious; no temptation "to do something about it" by way of rousing the attention, applying the mind, making an effort. She knows her business is to receive, to be moved, to be carried. It seems to her that her capacity is so filled as to leave scarcely room for other experiences; there is only sufficient attention and room for what she has to do in her daily round.

—*GMP*, 120, 121–23, 125–27, 128–29, 133, 136, 138–39

Only those who really allow God to make Christ Jesus their wisdom and their holiness can know unshakeable security. Relying on nothing whatsoever within themselves or anything created, they can never be let down. They are free. . . .

... [O]ur inmost heart rests always in the eye of the storm. We are spared nothing of life's burdens; shed tears as others do. We too can feel stretched to our limits and beyond, but all the while, that which is deepest in us is with God. Divine Love continually upholds the fragile creature that has risked all for its sake. This is, I believe, the perfection of faith: a divine empowering, a divine sustaining, and a divine holding. Consciousness may know only what natural knowledge knows, but holy Mystery is Home.   —*LM*, 111–12

TOTALLY FOR OTHERS

Those who have been transformed into the gift of God are oriented totally to others. Utterly conformed to Jesus, they have been taken completely into the Trinitarian life of self-giving love. Rachel speaks of the ones at the summit of the spiritual life as being bearers of living knowledge of the divine life, and channels through which God's love inundates creation.

To become Jesus in the mystical marriage is to be taken most deeply into this mystery of passionate Love, to be oneself a vehicle for this Love. Jesus, come to us in the Spirit, living Fire which would burn us up in love, is present in the world only insofar as men and women yield themselves up to him, are transformed in him, become Fire in him. The mystical marriage is not a state of psychic bliss, not a comprehensible fulfillment. It is utterly remote from such paltriness; it has nothing to do with self-states. It is to be with Jesus a total "for-Godness" which must mean being totally for others; it is an ecstasy of devotedness with no concern for self; it is to be Fire on earth, purifying, enkindling others at a depth far below what we can discern. We have insisted throughout that the direct action of God in the human being is wholly secret. It can be known only by its effects and even these are not easily assessed by "flesh and blood." "Life hidden with Christ in God" is nourished only by "life hidden with Christ in

God." It is those who are totally hidden and lost in God, living only with the life of Christ who are Fire on earth.

—*ICE*, 117–18

We are like windows: divine light—the natural presence of God—is there always beating on the panes, but the panes are dirty, so dirty that the light cannot penetrate. Our task is very simple indeed. . . . We do not have to make the sun shine, we have not to create our little suns, all we have to do is let the sun in and this we accomplish by cleaning the windows. When they are free from every stain the pure unadulterated light pours in. Then the window cannot be seen; it is all one with the light and, in its own way, has become light and light-giving. —*AL*, 76

Holiness implies a deep knowledge of God. It is union with God, a union of love, and love always means knowledge. Scripture over and over again testifies to this profound knowledge of God in those who are close to him. No longer servants but friends; Jesus' own knowledge of his Father is communicated to them; they are no longer dependent on signs and figures, parables, but can receive a direct revelation emanating from his presence. It does not imply "insights"; it is at a level below the conscious mind. What can be conceptualized is not it but may be an effect of it. It is as with a vast, deep lake, clasped and hidden in the bosom of a mountain. No one would know of its presence save the mountain which holds it were it not for the streams breaking through the mountain-side and cascading down into the valleys. From the deep inner source of knowledge light is shed on individual data; what is understood can be verbalized. However, the knowledge itself is beyond conceptualization; it is not of things, even holy things, but of God himself. It is one thing with union. It is the wisdom Paul speaks of, a communication of the Spirit of God who alone knows the depths of God. It is this Spirit who enlightens Jesus, revealing to him the mind of the Father, and Jesus' mind is ours. —*TBJ*, 100

I cannot imagine how any thoughtful reader could fail to be
impressed by St. Teresa [of Avila]'s writings even though he does
not find them attractive, even though he finds himself bewildered,
perhaps "put off." They ring with authenticity. Here is a woman
who surely *knows*. She isn't merely speculating, deducing; she
isn't relying on what others have said. Here is one with a well
of living knowledge within her and it is from this she is drawing
all the time. Her complete certainty is overwhelming, (and that
in spite of the inevitable emotional insecurity that must attend
our mortal state), she knows, she is certain, that what Jesus was
proclaiming, what Paul, John, and others have tried to express
of man's ultimate destiny of being with Christ in God, one spirit
with him who is Spirit, has become, even in this life, a living
reality in her. For her, it is no longer a matter of being called to
it, being on the way to it. For her it has happened; the kingdom
of God has come in her in its overpowering, transforming truth,
and she tells us, as John of the Cross will likewise tell us, that
this is true of few in their earthly sojourn. Teresa is aware that
she has a living knowledge known to few and that she is called
to communicate this knowledge to others: a wholly new dimension of human existence which can never be known theoretically
but only by moving into it and living there. It is that which eye
has not seen, nor ear heard and what the heart of man cannot
conceive.   —*ICE*, 1–2

Carmelites have no external apostolate. It is our faith-informed
conviction that a life given wholly to God is the most effective
apostolate. One for whom God matters supremely and who is
deeply concerned for others, keenly aware that love for God is
inseparable from love of the neighbor, will not find acceptance
of this apparent non-contribution easy. It will demand a constant reaffirmation of faith in her own vocation if she is to resist
the temptation to compensate in some way. It might not be so
difficult to accept if one had a sense of doing one's own job
well, of being a successful pray-er! This is unlikely. What happens if we feel we do not pray, that our prayer is hardly prayer,

so poverty-stricken it is, so lacking in all comforting feedback, all high sentiment? How often one hears the anxiety voiced: "I feel I do nothing for God. As a person vowed to a life of prayer I am a failure," and so forth. Now this, I believe, is where we touch the very heart of our vocation in the Church, the point where it bears witness to the truth that all must come from God, that all is pure gift and that as human beings we are there only to receive Love, to be "done unto" in gracious mercy and love. It is in this way that we glorify the pure, totally gratuitous love of God. Unless every Christian's heart lies thus at the feet of divine Love, humbly waiting, trusting, claiming nothing, relying only on what Love will do—the Love which has shown itself as such in Jesus—he or she may be religious, but not truly Christian. A Carmelite is called to live out this human vocation—synonymous with the Christian vocation—in an absolute way, becoming a glad receptivity for all that comes to her in a radical renunciation of every spiritual claim, every reassurance coming from the self. Thus it reminds us all of what is the heart of the matter. It is no easy vocation. I recall how, as a young Religious, suffering acutely from the feeling that as a Carmelite I was an utter failure, having nothing whatever to offer to God, I gradually perceived this to be precisely what the vocation is about, its very heart. I was to receive and to believe I had received without any token thereof. I was to accept to have nothing to give, to live always with empty hands. My giving could only be in allowing God to give. I recall with emotion and deep gratitude how I found this insight wonderfully confirmed by Thérèse [of Lisieux] in her letters, an English translation of which had just been published. Since then it has grown until it has taken over completely, and I realize how careful we must be, if we would be true to our vocation, not to evade, not to seek in anyway to overcome this profound awareness of spiritual inadequacy or pretend it is not there. The form of "saintliness" that held glamour for the contemporaries of St. Thérèse is hardly likely to be ours; but we shall not lack the urge to find ways and means of somehow making the life-style more interesting and ourselves more satisfactory, of "doing it better." Perhaps our lure today lies in constant discussions about it, in unrealistic ideas of ongoing formation, in more obvious involvement in Church affairs, in stimulating mental and emotional awareness of the world's sorrows. Obviously these must have their place; but everything depends on the motivation, in what we are hoping to achieve by them. Nothing must be allowed to take from us or even to mitigate our poverty, our helplessness, our "nothingness."

This is not a lovely spiritual ideal, but an experienced reality that can be loved and must be loved only because it opens ourselves and the world to the purifying, transforming, beatifying love of God.   —EP, 193–95

Complete Works of Ruth Burrows

BOOKS

Ascent to Love: The Spiritual Teaching of St. John of the Cross. London: Darton, Longman and Todd, 1987. Denville, NJ: Dimension, 1992.

Before the Living God. London: Sheed and Ward, 1975. New ed., with Introduction by Rowan Williams, London: Continuum, 2008. Mahwah, NJ: Paulist, 2008.

Carmel: Interpreting a Great Tradition. Foreword by Peter Smith. Preface by Roger Spencer. London: Sheed and Ward, 2000. Starrucca, PA: Dimension, 2000.

Essence of Prayer. Foreword by Wendy Beckett. London: Burns and Oates, 2006. Mahwah, NJ: Paulist, 2006.

Guidelines for Mystical Prayer. Foreword by B. C. Butler. London: Sheed and Ward, 1976. Denville, NJ: Dimension, 1980. New ed., London: Continuum, 2007. Mahwah, NJ: Paulist, 2017.

Interior Castle Explored: St. Teresa's Teaching on the Life of Deep Union with God. London: Sheed and Ward, 1981. New ed., London: Continuum, 2007. Mahwah, NJ: Paulist, 2007.

Letters on Prayer: An Exchange on Prayer and Faith. With Mark Allen. London: Sheed and Ward, 1999.

Living in Mystery. Introduction by Wendy Beckett. London: Sheed and Ward, 1996.

Living Love: Meditations on the New Testament. London: Darton, Longman and Todd, 1985. Denville, NJ: Dimension, 1985.

Love Unknown: Archbishop of Canterbury's Lent Book 2012. Foreword by Rowan Williams. London: Continuum, 2011.

Our Father: Meditations on the Lord's Prayer. London: Darton, Longman and Todd, 1986. Denville, NJ: Dimension, 1986.

Through Him, with Him, in Him: Meditations on the Liturgical Seasons. London: Sheed and Ward, 1987. Denville, NJ: Dimension, 1987.

To Believe in Jesus. London: Sheed and Ward, 1978. New ed., London: Continuum, 2010. Mahwah, NJ: Paulist, 2010.

The Watchful Heart: Daily Readings with Ruth Burrows. Introduced and edited by Elizabeth Ruth Obbard. London: Darton, Longman and Todd, 1988.

ARTICLES AND OTHER SHORT PIECES

"Alone with Him Alone." *Mount Carmel* 47, no. 2 (Autumn 1999): 3–6.

"Amen: The Human Response to God." *The Way* 43, no. 2 (April 2004): 78–90.

"Carmel: A Dream of the Spirit." *Mount Carmel* 34, no. 1 (Spring 1986): 47–50.

"Carmel: A Stark Encounter with the Human Condition." *The Way Supplement* 89 (Summer 1997): 97–105.

"Christian Prayer." *Mount Carmel* 38, no. 3 (Autumn 1990): 117–21.

"Come Lord Jesus." *Mount Carmel* 33, no. 3 (Autumn 1985): 166–70.

"The Crucifixion." *The Tablet*, March 12, 2005, 7.

"The Desert and the City." Review of *The Wilderness of God*, by Andrew Louth. *The Tablet*, September 28, 1991, 1180–81.

"Elizabeth of the Trinity." *Bible Alive* (August 1999): 9–16.

Foreword. In *Holy Daring: The Fearless Trust of Saint Thérèse of Lisieux*, by John Udris. Herefordshire, UK: Gracewing, 1997.

Foreword. In *Lamps of Fire: Daily Readings with St. John of the Cross*. Introduced and edited by Elizabeth Ruth Obbard. London: Darton, Longman and Todd, 1985.

Foreword. In *Living Water: Daily Readings with St. Teresa of Avila*. Introduced and edited by Mary Eland. London: Darton, Longman and Todd, 1985.

Foreword. In *Search for Nothing*, by Richard P. Hardy. London: Darton, Longman and Todd, 1987.

"Fully Human, Fully Alive." *Bible Alive* (January 2011): 4–9.

"The Gift of Understanding." *Mount Carmel* 33, no. 2 (Summer 1985): 83–86.

"Growth in Prayer." *The Way* 23, no. 4 (October 1983): 255–63.

"I Felt a Complete Failure, but I Hung on to God Even So." Interview by Bess Twiston Davies. *Times* (London), January 20, 2012, 88–89.

"If You Knew the Gift of God." *Priests and People* 11, no. 3 (March 1997): 87–90.

"Initial Prayer within the Carmelite Tradition." *Mount Carmel* 48, no. 3 (October–December 2000): 14–18.

Introduction. In *The Wisdom of St. Teresa of Avila*. Oxford: Lion Publishing, 1998.

"I Was Naked and You Gave Me Clothing." *The Tablet*, August 28, 2010, 10.

"Kindling the Fire of Prayer." Review of *Prayers for this Life*, edited by Christopher Howse. *The Tablet*, July 23, 2005, 22.

"Lose Yourself: Getting Past 'Me' to 'Thee.'" *America*, December 23, 2013, 19–20.

"Mary and the Apostles Pray for the Coming of the Holy Spirit." In *Journeying with Jesus: Personal Reflections on the Stations of the Cross and Resurrection*, edited by Lucy Russell, 109–12. Mowbray Lent Book 2013. London: Bloomsbury, 2012.

"Prayer in an Easter Community." *Priests and People* 17, no. 4 (April 2003): 138–42.

"Prayer in the Trinity." *Priests and People* 13, no. 4 (April 1999): 129–32.

"Prayer Is God's Work." Interview by Amy Frykholm. *Christian Century*, April 4, 2012, 10–11.

Review of *St. John of the Cross: Life and Thought of a Christian Mystic*, by Alain Cugno. *Mount Carmel* 31, no. 1 (Spring 1983): 51–55 (as "Sr Rachel").

Reviews of *Listening to Silence: An Anthology of Carthusian Writings*, edited by Robin Bruce Lockhart, and *Interior Prayer: They Speak by Silences* and *Where Silence Is Praise*, by a Carthusian. *Priests and People* 13, no. 3 (March 1999): 123–24.

"Signed with the Cross." *The Tablet*, December 14, 1991, 1541–42.

"Smile though Your Heart Is Aching." *The Tablet*, April 19, 2014, 10–11.

"Some Reflections on Prayer." *Mount Carmel* 43, no. 1 (April–June 1995): 6–12.

"Soul on Fire." Review of *The Impact of God*, by Iain Matthew. *The Tablet*, September 23, 1995, 1208.

"St. Thérèse of Lisieux and the Holy Child." *Priests and People* 15, no. 2 (December 2001): 448–51.

"Surrender Gratefully to Love." *The Tablet*, June 10, 2006, 12–13.

"Sustained Passion." *Mount Carmel* 30, no. 3 (Autumn 1982): 135–48.

"The Way to Perfection." *The Tablet*, October 16, 1982, 1032–33.

"Where I Can Best Give Myself Wholly to God." Interview by Sam Hailes. Eden, May 16, 2012. https://www.eden.co.uk/

UNPUBLISHED MATERIAL

"A Surpassing Gift of Grace." Quidenham, 1972.

"Manuscript." Quidenham. (Document comprised of the passages omitted from the published version of *Before the Living God*).

"On Formation." Quidenham.

Quis Ut Deus? Who Is as God? Meditations on the Kenosis of the Son of God. Quidenham, 2013.

"Rule of Carmel for Quidenham." Quidenham, 1993.

MODERN SPIRITUAL MASTERS
Robert Ellsberg, Series Editor

This series introduces the essential writing and vision of some of the great spiritual teachers of our time. While many of these figures are rooted in long-established traditions of spirituality, others have charted new, untested paths. In each case, however, they have engaged in a spiritual journey shaped by the challenges and concerns of our age. Together with the saints and witnesses of previous centuries, these modern spiritual masters may serve as guides and companions to a new generation of seekers.

Etty Hillesum (edited by Annemarie S. Kidder)
Caryll Houselander (edited by Wendy M. Wright)
Pope John XXIII (edited by Jean Maalouf)
Rufus Jones (edited by Kerry Walters)
Clarence Jordan (edited by Joyce Hollyday)
Walter Kasper (edited by Patricia C. Bellm and Robert A. Krieg)
John Main (edited by Laurence Freeman)
James Martin (edited by James T. Keane)
Anthony de Mello (edited by William Dych, S.J.)
Thomas Merton (edited by Christine M. Bochen)
John Muir (edited by Tim Flinders)
John Henry Newman (edited by John T. Ford, C.S.C.)
Henri Nouwen (edited by Robert A. Jonas)
Flannery O'Connor (edited by Robert Ellsberg)
Karl Rahner (edited by Philip Endean)
Brother Roger of Taizé (edited by Marcello Fidanzio)
Richard Rohr (edited by Joelle Chase and Judy Traeger)
Oscar Romero (by Marie Dennis, Rennie Golden, and Scott Wright)
Joyce Rupp (edited by Michael Leach)
Albert Schweitzer (edited by James Brabazon)
Frank Sheed and Maisie Ward (edited by David Meconi)
Jon Sobrino (edited by Robert Lassalle-Klein)
Sadhu Sundar Singh (edited by Charles E. Moore)
Mother Maria Skobtsova (introduction by Jim Forest)
Dorothee Soelle (edited by Dianne L. Oliver)
Jon Sobrino (edited by Robert Lasalle-Klein)
Edith Stein (edited by John Sullivan, O.C.D.)
David Steindl-Rast (edited by Clare Hallward)
William Stringfellow (edited by Bill Wylie-Kellerman)
Pierre Teilhard de Chardin (edited by Ursula King)
Mother Teresa (edited by Jean Maalouf)
St. Thérèse of Lisieux (edited by Mary Frohlich)
Phyllis Tickle (edited by Jon M. Sweeney)
Henry David Thoreau (edited by Tim Flinders)
Howard Thurman (edited by Mary Krohlich)
Leo Tolstoy (edited by Charles E. Moore)
Evelyn Underhill (edited by Emilie Griffin)
Vincent Van Gogh (by Carol Berry)
Jean Vanier (edited by Carolyn Whitney-Brown)
Swami Vivekananda (edited by Victor M. Parachin)
Simone Weil (edited by Eric O. Springsted)
John Howard Yoder (edited by Paul Martens and Jenny Howells)